The Book of Fasting

A HANAFI GUIDE TO SIYĀM
BASED ON QUR'AN, SUNNAH,
AND CLASSICAL SOURCES

The Book of Fasting

A HANAFI GUIDE TO SIYĀM BASED ON QUR'AN, SUNNAH, AND CLASSICAL SOURCES

Muhammad ibn al-Hasan al-Shaybani and other early Hanafi jurists

1 2 3 4 5 6 7 8 9 10

All rights reserved. No part of this publication may be reproduced, stored in a retrieval system or transmitted in any form or by any means – electronic, mechanical, photocopying, recording or otherwise – without written permission from the publisher.

© Light Publishing 2025

Muhammad ibn al-Hasan al-Shaybani
and other early Hanafi jurists

The Book of Fasting

ISBN 978-1-915570-50-5

www.lightpublishing.co.uk

بِسْمِ اللَّهِ الرَّحْمَٰنِ الرَّحِيمِ

CONTENTS

Chapter 1: The Importance of Fasting   11
    The virtue of fasting   12
    The objectives of fasting   13

Chapter 2: Sighting the Moon   15
    If the horizon is clear   16
    If the horizon is not clear   16
    If someone alone sees the crescent   17
    People travelling   17
    Considerations of difference in location   17
    Astronomical calculations   18
    The size of the crescent   18
    The day of doubt   18
    Follow the *jama'ah*   19

Chapter 3: A description of Fasting   21
    The *fards* in fasting   21
    The Sunnahs of fasting   24
    Suhur   24
    Iftar   25
    With what should one break the fast?   26
    Reading the Qur'an   27
    Du'a   27
    Refraining from sins and vain pursuits   28

Chapter 4: The Fasting of Ramadan   29
    When was fasting made obligatory?   30
    The virtues of the month of Ramadan   31
    The sin of not fasting during Ramadan   32
    The wisdom behind fixing days for fasting   32
    On whom the fasting is obligatory   33
    The fasting of children   33

Women in a state of menstruation	34
The invalid and the traveller	35
Those physically unable to fast	37
Nafl fast	38
The six days of *Shawwal*	39
The Day of 'Arafah	39
'Ashura'	40
Fasting on Mondays and Thursdays	40
Three days of every month	41
Fasting on alternate days	42
When voluntary fasting becomes compulsory	42

Chapter 5: Days when Fasting is Forbidden or Disliked — 43

Forbidden days	43
Disliked days	44
Day of doubt	44
Friday	44
Saturday	44
Wisaal	45
The whole year	46
Fasting without the consent of one's husband	46

Chapter 6: What is Allowed during Fasting — 49

Eating and drinking forgetfully	49
Tasting the food	49
Getting up in the morning as *junubi*	49
Kissing	50
Wet dream	51
Applying oil	52
Cooling with water	52
Applying *kuhl*	52
Injection	53
Cupping	53
Using *miswak* or toothpaste	53

Chapter 7: What Breaks the Fast — 55

What makes both *qada'* and *kaffarah* compulsory?	55
Smoking	56
What necessitates *qada'* only?	57

Breaking the fast by mistake	57
Breaking the fast for medical reasons	57
Sexual contact that is less than *jima'*	57
Vomiting deliberately	58
Eating something which is not food	58
Breaking a fast other than during the month of Ramadan	58
Delaying the *qada'*	59
Separation between *qada'* fasts	59

Chapter 8: The Night of al-Qadr — 61
Seeking the Night of *al-Qadr* — 61
Which night is it? — 62
Worship during this night — 64

Chapter 9: I'tikaf — 65
Types of *i'tikaf* — 66
Wajib i'tikaf — 66
Sunnah *I'tikaf* — 66
Mustahabb I'tikaf — 67
Conditions for the validity of *I'tikaf* — 67
Time — 68
When one should go for the Sunnah *I'tikaf* — 69
Specifying a place for the *mu'takif* — 60
What one should do during *i'tikaf* — 70
What is allowed for the *mu'takif* — 70
What invalidates the *i'tikaf* — 70
Qada' of *i'tikaf* — 71

Chapter 1

THE IMPORTANCE OF FASTING

THE WORD FOR fasting in Arabic is *sawm*. Literally it means 'abstaining from'. As an Islamic term, *sawm* means abstaining from eating, drinking, and sexual intercourse from dawn to sunset. Fasting is an effective means for the purification of the soul, for strengthening the discipline of desire and self-control. Like *salah* and *zakah*, it has been part of God's religion from the very beginning. The Qur'an says: *"O you who have believed, decreed upon you is fasting as it was decreed upon those before you that you may become righteous ".*¹ Fasting strengthens one's fear of Allah, morality and self-control and deepens one's consciousness of Allah.

The fact that fasting is a means to moral elevation is evident because Allah not only imposes checks upon eating, drinking and sexual intercourse from dawn to sunset, but also exhorts His slaves to refrain lies, etc. Abu Hurayrah narrated: The Prophet ﷺ said, "Whoever does not give up forged speech and evil actions, Allah is not in need of his leaving his food and drink".²

During the month of Ramadan the whole atmosphere is permeated with piety and devotion to Allah. There is one extra congregational prayer, *Tarawih*, offered during the night, in which the Qur'an is recited and Muslims are reminded of the fact that it was during the month of Ramadan that the revelation of the Qur'an commenced. *Sadaqah* is also given with greater zeal and fervour during this month. In this way, the whole Muslim society is inspired with the love of Allah. Abu Hurayrah reported from Allah's Messenger ﷺ as saying: "When Ramadan begins, the gates of Heaven are opened, the gates of Hell are locked, and the devils are chained".³

---

1 Al-Baqarah 183.
2 Al-Bukhari, k. al-sawm, b. man lam yada' qawl al-zur.
3 Al-Bukhari, k. al-sawm, b. hal yuqalu ramadan; Muslim, k. al-siyam, b. fadl shahr ramadan.

THE VIRTUE OF FASTING

Since fasting is of such great importance in Islam, The Prophet ﷺ encouraged believers in many ways to observe both the obligatory and the voluntary fasting. Abu Hurayrah narrated that the Messenger of Allah ﷺ said: "Fasting is a shield. Therefore, the person fasting should avoid talking about desire and should not behave foolishly and impudently, and if somebody fights with him or abuses him, he should tell him, 'I am fasting". The Prophet ﷺ added, "By Him in Whose Hands my soul is, the smell coming out from the mouth of a fasting person is better with Allah than the smell of musk. Allah says about the fasting person, 'He has left his food< drink and desires for My sake. The fast is for Me. So I will reward (the fasting person) for it and the reward of good deeds is multiplied ten times".[4]

Sahl ibn Sa'd narrated that the Prophet ﷺ said: "There is a gate in Paradise called al-Rayyan, and those who observe fasts will enter through it on the Day of Resurrection and none except them will enter through it. It will be said, 'Where are those who used to observe fasts?' They will get up, and none except them will enter through it. After their entry, the gate will be closed and nobody will enter through it".[5]

Abu Hurayrah narrates that the Messenger of Allah ﷺ said: "Whoever gives two kinds (of things or property) in charity for Allah's Cause, will be called from the gates of Paradise and will be addressed, 'O slaves of Allah here is prosperity'. So, whoever was amongst the people who used to offer their prayers, will be called from the gate of the prayer; and whoever was amongst the people who used to participate in *jihad*, will be called from the gate of *jihad*, and whoever was amongst those who used to observe fasts, will be called from the gate of al-Rayyan; whoever was amongst those who used to give in charity, will be called from the gate of charity". Abu Bakr said: "Let my parents be sacrificed for you, O Allah's Apostle. No distress or need will befall him who will be called from those gates. Will there be any one who will be called from all these gates?' The Prophet ﷺ replied: 'Yes, and I hope you will be among them'."[6]

---

4   Al-Bukhari, *k. al-sawm, b. hal yaqulu inna sa'im idha shutima*; Muslim, *k. al-siyaam, b. fadl al-siyaam.*
5   Al-Bukhari, *k. bad' al-khalq, b. sifat abwab al-jannah*; Muslim, *k. al-siyam, b. fadl al-siyam.*
6   Al-Bukhari, *k. al-sawm, b. al-rayyan li al-sa'imin;* Muslim, *k. al-zakah, b. man jama'a al-sadaqah wa a'mal al-birr.*

THE OBJECTIVES OF FASTING

The purpose of fasting has been described by Allah Himself. Allah, Exalted is He, says: "*O you who have believed, decreed upon you is fasting as it was decreed upon those before you that you may become righteous*". [7] Abu Hurayrah narrated that the Messenger of Allah ﷺ said: "Fasting is a shield. So, the person observing fast should not use obscene language and should not behave foolishly and impudently, and if somebody fights with him or abuses him, he should tell him twice, 'I am fasting'."[8]

Imam Ghazali remarks: "The object of fasting is that man should produce within him a semblance of the Divine Attribute of *Samadiyyah* (being above lower things), that he should, as far as possible, take after the angels and cast off the beastly propensities because the angels are free from desire and the place of man too is above the animal and he has, further, been given the power of discrimination to resist the pressure of inordinate appetites. He is, of course, inferior to angels in the sense that desire often overpowers him and he has to strive hard to subdue it. When he succumbs to sensual propensities he degenerates into the lowliest of the low and joins the herds of cattle when he conquers them he attains the dizzy heights of the heavenly host and begins to dwell on the plane of the angels".[9]

Emphasising the same point Imam Ibn al-Qayyim says: "The purpose of fasting is that the spirit of man is released from the clutches of desire and moderation prevails in his carnal self, and, through it, he realises the goal of purification and everlasting felicity. It is aimed at curtailing the intensity of desire and lust by means of hunger and thirst, at inducing man to realise how many were there in the world like him who had to go even without a small quantity of food, at making it difficult for the devil to deceive him, and at restraining his organs from turning towards things in which there was the loss of both the worlds. Fasting, thus, is the bridle of the God-fearing, the shield of the crusaders and the discipline of the virtuous .... Fasting is most efficacious in the protection of the external limbs and internal organs. It guards against disorders resulting from the accumulation of effete matter. It

---

7 *Al-Baqarah* 183.
8 Al-Bukhari, *k. al-sawm, b. hal yaqulu inna sa'im idha shutima*; Muslim, *k. al-siyam, b.fadl al-siyam*.
9 Al-Ghazali, *Ihya' 'ulum al-din*, i. 332.

expels the toxins that are injurious to health and cures the ailments which develop in the body due to over-indulgence. It is beneficial for health and most helpful in leading a life of piety and good-doing ... Hence, a person who wishes to marry but does not have the means to support a family is advised to observe fasting. It has been prescribed as a sovereign remedy for him, the purpose being to demonstrate that since the advantages of fasting were evident from the point of view of common sense Allah has enjoined it as an act of mercy for the protection of His slaves".[10]

Shah Waliullah writes: "There are two ways of reduction in diet. One is to eat sparingly and the other is to observe such a long interval between meals that the object of curtailment is gained. In the Shari'ah the latter course has been prescribed because it induces an adequate appreciation of the torments of hunger and thirst and strikes at the root of the carnal appetites, a definite reduction in whose force and intensity is noticed. On the contrary, in the former case, these results are not obtained owing to the continuity of meals. Besides, it is not possible to lay down a general rule for reduction as the circumstances differ from one individual to another. One person may manage on half the quantity of food that another needs. Thus, if a general limit is laid down for everyone, one will profit by it and the other will suffer .... it, again, was desirable, that the hours of fasting were not so long as to entail unbearable hardship as, for instance, three days and three nights. Apart from being opposed to the spirit of the Shari'ah, it would also have generally been impracticable ... It was necessary that the opportunity to abjure food and drink occurred repeatedly and in succession in order that it could serve the purpose of an exercise in submission. To go without food only would avail nothing".[11]

---

10 Ibn al-Qayyim, *Zad al-ma'ad*, ii. 28-30.
11 al-Dihlawi, *Hujjatullah al-balighah*, ii. 76.

Chapter 2

SIGHTING THE MOON

THE ISLAMIC CALENDAR, like many other religious calendars is a lunar calendar. The beginning of the month is marked by sighting the crescent. As soon as the crescent is sighted the month has started and it will continue until the sighting of the next crescent. Thus, a lunar month will either be a 29 days or 30 days. 'Abdullah ibn 'Umar reported from Allah's Messenger ﷺ who said: "The month is thus, and thus, and thus, and he flapped his hands with all their fingers twice. But at the third turn, he folded his right thumb or left thumb (in order to give an idea of 29)".[12] In another version of the same hadith, Allah's Messenger ﷺ said: "The month is thus and thus (he then withdrew his thumb at the third time)" . He then said: "Fast when you see it, and break your fast when you see it, and if the weather is cloudy calculate it as 30 days".[13]

People must look for the new moon on the 29th of the month of Sha'ban and if they sight it, then they fast, but if it is hidden from their sight, then they complete the number of days for Sha'ban, that is 30, then they start fasting. 'A'ishah narrated that the Apostle of Allah ﷺ used to count the days in Sha'ban in a manner he did not count any other month; then he fasted when he sighted the new moon of Ramadan; but if the weather was cloudy he counted 30 days and then fasted".[14] 'Abdullah ibn 'Umar reported that the Messenger of Allah ﷺ mentioned Ramadan and said: "Do not fast unless you see the crescent (of Ramadan), and do not give up fasting until you see the crescent (of Shawwal), but if the sky is overcast, then act on estimation (i.e. count Sha'ban as 30 days)".[15]

---

12   al-Bukhari, *k. al-sawm, b. qawl al-nabi sallallahu 'alayhi wa sallam idha ra'aytum al-hilala fasumu;* Muslim, *k. alsiyam, b. wujub sawm ramadan li ru'yat al-hilal.*
13   Ibid
14   Abu Dawud, *k. al-sawm, b. idha ughmiya al-shahr.*
15   al-Bukhari, *k. al-sawm, b. qawl al-nabi sallallahu 'alayhi wa sallam idha ra'aytum*

Imam Muhammad says after narrating this hadith: "We adhere to this and this is the opinion of Abu Hanifah".[16]

If the horizon is clear

If the horizon is clear and there is no dust or cloud in the sky, then the testimony of one or two people is not accepted until a large group – whose report establishes certain knowledge – sights it.[17]

If the horizon is not clear

If there is some reason, for not being able to see the moon, such a cloud of dust in the sky, then the testimony of one just person's sighting of the new moon of Ramadan irrespective of whether it is a man or a woman will be accepted. [18] 'Abdullah ibn 'Umar narrated that the people looked for the moon, so I informed the Apostle of Allah ﷺ that I had sighted it. He fasted and commanded the people to fast".[19]

'Abdullah ibn 'Abbas narrated that a Bedouin came to the Prophet ﷺ and said: "I have sighted the moon, that is, of Ramadan. He (the Prophet ﷺ), asked: 'Do you testify that there is no God but Allah?' He replied: 'Yes'. He again asked: 'Do you testify that Muhammad is the Apostle of Allah? He replied: 'Yes'. And he testified that he had sighted the moon. The Prophet ﷺ said: 'Bilal, announce to the people that they must fast tomorrow'."[20]

As for the sighting of the crescent of Shawwal when the horizon is not clear, the *imam* will not accept the testimony of one person; rather there should be the testimony of two just males or one male and two females.[21] 'Ali says: "When two just men bear the testimony of sighting the crescent, then break the fast".[22]

---

al-hilala fasumu; Muslim, k. al-siyam, b.wujub sawm ramadan li ru'yat al-hilal.
16 Muhammad, *al-Muwatta'*, 122.
17 al-Samarqandi, *Tuhfat al-fuqaha'* 165.
18 Ibid.
19 Abu Dawud, k. al-sawm, b. shahadat al-wahid 'ala ru'yat hilal ramadan
20 Al-Tirmidhi, k. al-sawm, b. ma ja'a fi al-sawm bi al-shahadah; Abu Dawud, k. al-sawm, b. shahadat wahid 'ala ru'yat hilal ramadan, al-Nasa'I, k. al-siyam, b. qabul shahadat al-rajul al-wahid 'ala hilal shahr ramadan; Ibn Majah, k. al-siyam, b. ma ja'a fi al-shahadah 'ala ru'yat hilal.
21 al-Samarqandi, *Tuhfat al-fuqaha'* 165.
22 Ibn Abi Shaybah, *al-Musannaf*, vi. 257.

If someone alone sees the crescent
Whoever sees the new moon of Ramadan when alone, should fast even if the imam does not accept his testimony.[23]

Whoever sees the new moon marking the *fitr*, i.e the end of the fast when alone, he should not break his fast; rather, he should continue fasting with the community.[24]

People travelling
If one travels to a place where the month of Ramadan started later, one continues fasting with the people as long as the number of one's fast does not exceed 30 days. If the people of the locality continue fasting and one has completed 30 fasts, one should stop fasting, and must wait and pray *'id* with them. The reason for this is that the lunar month cannot last longer than 30 days.

If someone travels to a place where the people started their fast earlier, then one has to do *'id* with them, and does not need to do any *qada'* (to perform an act of worship after one has missed its prescribed time) as long as one has fasted 29 days. If one's fast was less than 29 days then one has to do *qada'* until it becomes 29 days, because there is no month lasting less than 29 days.

CONSIDERATION OF DIFFERENCE IN LOCATION

According to the most sound opinion, differences in location are not considered. If people of a particular place do not sight the moon, but they receive reliable information from any quarter where the sighting has been established legally, then they should follow it.[25] Ibn al-Mundhir says: "Most jurists say when it is affirmed by the report of the people that the people of any town have sighted it before them, then they have to do *qada*" of the day that they did not fast; this is the opinion of Malik, Shafi'i, Ahmad and the people of *Ra'y* (Hanafis).[26]

---

23   al-Samarqandi, *Tuhfat al-fuqaha'* 165.
24   See: *al-Mawsili, al-Ikhtiyar lit a'lil al-mukhtar*, i. 168.
25   See: *Fatawa Mustafa al-Zarqa'* 170-171; al-Mawsili, *al-Iktiyar lit a'lil al-mukhtar*, i. 168.
26   al-Baghawi, *Sharh al-sunnah*, iii. 464.

ASTRONOMICAL CALCULATIONS

Astronomical calculations, being based on accurate computation, help in ascertaining the impossibly of sighting the crescent. The Muslim leader should reject any claim of sighting the moon while such sighting is deemed an astronomical impossibility.

THE SIZE OF THE CRESCENT

The beginning of the month is confirmed by sighting the crescent. If the crescent is not sighted on the 29th, and on the next night the crescent appears bigger than it would normally be on the first night, it is nevertheless counted as the first night of the new month. Abu al-Bakhtari reported: "We went out to perform *'umrah* and when we encamped in the valley of Naklah, we tried to sight the new moon. Some of the people said it was three nights old, and others said that it was two nights old. We then met 'Abdullah ibn 'Abbas and told him we had seen the new moon, but that some of the people said it was three nights old and others that it was two nights old. He asked on which night we had seen it; and when we told him we had seen it on such and such night, he said the Prophet of Allah ﷺ had said: 'Allah deferred it till the time it is seen, so it is to be reckoned from the night you saw it'."[27]

THE DAY OF DOUBT

If it is cloudy or there is dust on the horizon, and people are to sight the crescent, then to fast the next day with the intention of Ramadan whilst in doubt is disliked.[28]

Abu Ishaq reported on the authority of Silah ibn Zufar who said: "We were with 'Ammar on the day when the appearance of the moon was doubtful. (The meat of a) goat was brought to him. Some people kept aloof from (eating) it. 'Ammar said: 'He who keeps fast on this day disobeys Abu al-Qasim (i.e. the Prophet) ﷺ'."[29] Hudhayfah narrated: "The Prophet ﷺ said: 'Do not fast (for Ramadan) before the coming of the month until you sight the moon or complete the number (30 days); then fast until you sight the moon or complete the number (of 30 days)."[30]

---

27 Muslim, *k. al-siyam, b. bayan annahu la I'tibar bikibar al-hilal wa sigharih.*
28 al-Kasani, Bada'I al-sana'I , ii. 562.
29 al-Bukhari, *k. al-sawm, b. qawl al-nabi sallallahu 'alayhi wa sallam idha ra'aytum al-hilala fasumu;* Abu Dawud, *k. al-siyam, b. karahiyat yawm al-shakk.*
30 al-Nasa'I, *k. al-siyam, dhikr al-ikhtilaf 'ala mansur.*

If the day of doubt is a day during which one used to do *nafl* (supererogatory) fasting, then one is allowed to fast. Abu Hurayrah narrates: "The Prophet ﷺ said: 'None of you should fast a day or two before the month of Ramadan unless he has the habit of fasting, then he can fast that day'."[31] 'Abdullah ibn 'Abbas narrates: "The Prophet ﷺ said: 'Do not fast one day or two days just before Ramadan except in the case of a man who has been in the habit of observing a fast (on that day); and do not fast until you sight it (the moon). Then fast until you sight it. If a cloud appears on that day (i.e. 29th of Ramadan) then complete the number (30 days) and then end the fasting: a month consists of 29 days."[32]

FOLLOW THE JAMA'AH

When there is confusion in any locality regarding the beginning of the month, people should follow the *jama'ah*. *Jama'ah* means a group of Muslims with a leader. If there is no leader, people must agree to select a leader on the basis of consultation, and then they should follow his decision. Once a decision is made by the *jama'ah* concerning the beginning of the month, then that is the beginning of the month and people are not allowed to follow their individual opinions in these collective matters. Abu Hurayrah narrates that the Prophet ﷺ said: "The fasting is the day the people fast, and the end of Ramadan is on the day when they end it, and the *'id* (festival) of sacrifice is on the day when they sacrifice".[33] The meaning of the hadith is that the fasting and 'id are done with the *jama'ah* and the majority of the people.[34]

---

[31] al-Bukhari, *k. al-sawm, b. la yataqaddamanna ramadan bi sawm yawm aw yawmayn;* Muslim, *k. al-siyam, b. la taqaddamu ramadan bi sawm yawm aw yawmayn.*

[32] Abu Dawud, *k. alsiyam, b. man qala fa in ghumma 'alaykym fasumu thalathin.*

[33] Abu Dawud, *k. al-sawm, b. idha akhta'a al-qawm al-hilal;* al-Tirmidhi, *k. al-sawm, b. ma ja'a al-sawm yawma tasumun.*

[34] al-Baghawi, *Sharh al-sunnah,* iii. 465.

Chapter 3

A DESCRIPTION OF FASTING

FASTING CONSISTS OF certain *fards* (a definitive obligation) acts and some *Sunnahs*, which are explained below:

THE *FARDS* IN FASTING
There are two *fards* in fasting:
1. Desisting from eating, drinking and sexual intercourse during the day, from daybreak to sunset. [35] Allah, Exalted is He, says: *"So now, have relations with them and seek that which Allah has decreed for you. And eat and drink until the white thread of dawn becomes distinct to you from the black thread [of night]. Then complete the fast until the sunset."*[36] White thread means light of the day, and black thread means the darkness of the night.

'Abdullah ibn 'Abbas while explaining the Qur'anic verse: *"O you who have believed, decreed upon you is fasting as it was decreed upon those before you that you may become righteous,"* said: "During the lifetime of the Prophet ﷺ when the people offered night prayer, they were asked to abstain from food and drink and (intercourse with) women, they kept fasting till the next night. A man betrayed himself and had intercourse with his wife after he had offered the night prayer, and he continued his fast. So Allah, Exalted is He, intended to make it (fasting) easy for the living. Thus providing a concession and benefit. Allah, the Glorified, said: *'Allah knows what you used to do secretly among yourselves'.* By this Allah benefited the people and provided concession and ease to them'."[37]

Al-Bara' narrated: "It was the custom among the Companions of Muhammad ﷺ when fasting and food was presented for them (for *iftar*-breaking of the fast), however, they fell asleep before eating, they

---

35   al-Samarqandi, *Tuhfat al-fuqaha'* 162.
36   *al-Baqarah* 187.
37   Abu Dawud, k. *al-siyam*, b. *mabda' fard al-siyam*.

would not eat that night and the following day until sunset. Qays ibn Sirmah al-Ansari was fasting and came to his wife at the time of *iftar* and asked her whether she had anything to eat. She replied: 'No, but I will go and bring some for you'. He used to do hard work during the day and so was overwhelmed by sleep and slept. When his wife came and saw him, she said: 'Disappointment for you'. When it was midday on the following day, he fainted. The Prophet ﷺ was informed about the whole matter and the following verses were revealed: *'You are permitted to go to your wives (for sexual relations) on the night of fasting'.* So, they were overjoyed by it. And then Allah also revealed: *'And eat and drink until the white thread of dawn appears to you distinct from the black thread, then complete your fasting till the nightfall'.*"[38]

'Adi ibn Hatim narrated: "When the verse *'Until the white thread appears to you, distinct from the black thread,'* was revealed, I took two (hair) strings, one black and the other white, and kept them under my pillow and went on looking at them throughout the night but could not make anything out of it. So, the next morning I went to the Messenger of Allah ﷺ and told him the whole story. He said to me: 'That verse means the darkness of the night and the whiteness of the dawn'."[39]

'Umar ibn al-khattab narrates: "The Messenger of Allah ﷺ said: 'When night falls from this side and the day vanishes from this side and the sun sets, then the fasting person should break his fast'".[40]

2. Making *niyyah* (intention) because fasting is an act of worship and all acts of worship require intention. Allah says: *"And they were not commanded, but to worship Allah, making the religion sincerely for Him"*.[41] The Prophet ﷺ said: "Every action is based upon intention. For everyone is that which he intended. Whoever made the migration is to Allah and His Prophet. Whoever's migration was to what he migrated to".[42] As a result of this verse and this hadith, all scholars agree that fasting, like any other act of worship, cannot be valid without intention.

Intention, as has been explained in the Book of Salah (*Al-Fiqh Al-Is-*

---

38 *al-Baqarah* 187.
39 Muslim, *k. al-siyam, b. bayan anna al-dukhula fi al-sawm yahsulu* ...
40 al- Bukhari, *k. al-sawm, b. mata yahillu fitr al-sa'im; Muslim, k. al-siyam, b. bayan waqt inqida' al-sawm wa khuruj al-nahar.*
41 Al- *Bayyinah* 5.
42 Al- Bukhari, *k. bad' al-wahy.*

Iami-Volume 1), is an act of the heart; one does not need to utter anything verbally. There are two timings for making intention depending on the types of fasts:

i. In the fasting of the *qada'*, *kaffarah* and vows of un-specified days, one must make intention before the dawn. All the scholars agreed on this. [43] Hafsah narrated that the Prophet ﷺ said: "The fasting of those who did not make their intention before the dawn is no fasting for them".[44]

ii. In the obligatory fasting of Ramadan, vows of fasting on specific days, and all *Sunnah and nafl* fasting, one can make intention any time from the night until before the *zawal* (midday, when the sun begins ton decline).[45] 'A'ishah narrated that: "The Prophet ﷺ used to come to me in the day and ask: 'Do you have any anything to eat?' I would say: 'No'. Then he would say: 'Then I am fasting'."[46] Umm al-Darda' narrates: "Abu al-Darda' would ask: 'Do you have food? If we said: 'No, he would reply: 'Then I am fasting'."[47] The same was the practise of Abu Talhah, Abu Hurayrah, 'Abdullah ibn 'Abbas and Hudhayfah.[48]

Those places where the days or nights are very long

In these places, nevertheless, within any period of 24 hours, both sunrise and sunset are witnessed. In such places, the period of fasting will be calculated in the usual way with respect to the sunrise and sunset. However, if doing so will lead to harm – severe illness or death – for a particular person, due to the length of the fast, it is permissible for that person not to fast while the risk of harm is present. Mere conjecture is not sufficient in this regard; rather, the individual must be almost certain that serious harm will result from fasting. This can be known from certain symptoms or from experience, or from the advice of a health professional who affirms that fasting will lead to severe illness or death or that it will aggravate an illness or endanger recovery from a previous

---

43 al-Baghawi, *Sharh al-sunnah*, iii. 476.
44 Abu Dawud, *k. al-sawm, b. al-niyyah fi al-siyam*; al-Tirmidhi, *k. al-sawm, b. ma ja'a la siyama li man lam ya'zim min al-layl*.
45 Al-Samarqandi, *Tuhfat al-fuqaha'* 167.
46 Muslim, *k. al-siyam, b, jawaz al-nafilah bi niyyatin min al-nahar qab al-zawal*.
47 Al-Baghawi, *Shah al- sunnah*, iii. 477.
48 ibid.

illness. Each person is different in this regard. Those people who leave fasting for such reasons should make up the missed fasts when they are able to do so.⁴⁹

In some of these places, the nights are so short that there is either no time or very little time for *'Isha'* Prayer because the twilight does not disappear. In this situation the time of the *suhur* (the pre-dawn meal) will be based on an estimate. The people resident in such places should consider what, in other seasons, the shortest period of time is between sunset and *'Isha'*, and between dawn and sunrise. That shortest period should then be taken as the norm for the season when the twilight does not disappear. In the United Kingdom, for example, if the shortest period between sunset and *'Isha'* is one and a quarter hours, and the shortest period between dawn and sunrise is one and half hours, then people should pray *'Isha'* and *Tarawih* in the difficult summer months one and a quarter hours after sunset, and they should finish the *suhur* one and half hours before sunrise.

Those places where the days or nights cannot be distinguished
Very exceptionally, Muslims may find themselves living temporarily in or passing through places where the sun hardly appears or disappears at all in some periods of the year. In such situations, the most practicable solution is to follow the prayer and fasting times of the nearest large town where Muslims are permanently resident.⁵⁰

THE SUNNAHS OF FASTING
There are certain *Sunnahs* and recommended matters which, once observed, fulfil the purpose of fasting. They are as follows:

SUHUR
Suhur is a meal which one eats before dawn when intending to fast. It is *Sunnah* to take *suhur* and the Prophet ﷺ has recommended it in many *ahadith*. Anas ibn Malik narrated that the Prophet ﷺ said: "Take *suhur* as there is a blessing in it".⁵¹ Al-'Irbad ibn Sariyah narrated: "The

---
49   See: *Fatawa al-Shaykh Makhluf*, i.272, *Majallat al-buhuth al-islamiyyah*, issue 25, p,32.
50   See: *Qararat majlis al-majma' al-fiqhi al-islami*, p. 91.
51   Al-Bukhari, k. al-sawm, b. barakat al-suhur min ghayr ijab; Muslim, k. fadl al-suhur.

Apostle of Allah ﷺ invited me to a meal shortly before dawn during the month of Ramadan saying: 'Come to the blessed morning meal'."[52] 'Amr ibn al-'As reported Allah's Messenger ﷺ as saying: "The difference between our fasting and that of the people of the Book is eating at the time of *suhur*".[53]

Its timing

The time of *suhur* is from midnight to the beginning of the *Fajr*. It is better to delay *suhur* so that one has *suhur* as close as possible to *Fajr*. Anas ibn Malik narrates that Zayd ibn Thabit said: "We had *suhur* with the Messenger of Allah ﷺ and then we stood up for the *(Fajr)* prayer'. Anas said: "I asked him how long the gap between *suhur* and the prayer was?" Zayd answered: "The amount needed to read 50 verses".[54]

'Abdullah ibn Mas'ud, 'Abdullah ibn 'Umar and 'A'ishah all narrated that Bilal used to pronounce the *adhan* at night, so the Messenger of Allah ﷺ said: "Carry on taking your meals (eat and drink) Until Ibn Umm Maktum pronounces the *adhan*, for he does not pronounce it till it is dawn".[55] Sahl ibn Sa'd reported: "I used to take my *suhur* meals with my family and then hurry up for presenting myself for the *(fajr)* prayer with Allah's Apostle".[56] Ibrahim al-Nakha'i says: "It is Sunnah to delay the *suhur*".[57] Mujahid says: "It is from the etiquettes of the Prophets to delay the *suhur*".[58]

IFTAR

Iftar means breaking the fast. It is Sunnah to break the fast as soon as the sun is set, and to delay it is disliked. Sahl ibn Sa'd narrated: "The Messenger of Allah ﷺ said:

'People will remail on the right path as long as they hasten the breaking of the fast'."[59] Abu Hurayrah narrated that Prophet ﷺ said:

---

52   Abu Dawud, *k. al-sawm, b. man samma al-suhur al-ghada'*; al-Nasa'I, *k. al-siyam, b. da'wat al-suhur.*
53   Muslim, *k. al-siyam, b.fadl al-suhur.*
54   Al-Bukhari, *k. mawaqit al-salah, b. waqt al-fajr*; Muslim, *k. al-siyam, b. fadl al-suhur.*
55   Muslim, *k. al-siyam, b. bayan anna al-dukhula fi al-sawm yahsulu ....*
56   al-Bukhari, *k. al-sawm, b. ta'jil al-suhur.*
57   Ibn Abi Shaybah, al-Musannaf, vi. 121.
58   Ibid., vi. 122.
59   al-Bukhari, *k. al-sawm, b. ta'jil al-iftar*; Muslim, *k. al-siyam, b. fadl al-suhur.*

"Religion will continue to prevail as long as people hasten to break the fast, because the Jews and the Christians delay doing so".[60] 'Abdullah ibn Abi Awfa reported: "We were with the Messenger of Allah ﷺ on a journey during the month of Ramadan. When the sun had sunk he said: 'So and so, get down (from your ride) and prepare the meal of parched barley for us'. He said: 'messenger of Allah, still (there is light of) day'. He (the Prophet) said: 'Get down and prepare the meal of parched barley and offered it to him, and the Apostle of Allah ﷺ drank that (liquid meal). He then with the gesture of his hand informed us that when the sun sank from that side and the night appeared from that side, then the observer of the fast should break it".[61]

Abu 'Atiyyah reported: "I and Mashreq went to 'Aishah and said to her: 'Mother of all Believers, there are two people among the Companions of Muhammad ﷺ, one among whom hastens in breaking the fast and in observing prayer', She said: 'Who among the two hastens in breaking the fast and observing prayers?' We said: 'It is Abdullah, (i.e. ibn Mas'ud) whereupon she said: "This is what the Messenger of Allah ﷺ did. Abu Kurayb added: "The second one was Abu Musa".[62] In another version of the hadith, the name of the first companion is mentioned as Hudhayfah rather than 'Abdullah. Imam Muhammad says: 'We adhere to the practice of Hudhayfah, and this is the opinion of Abu Hanifah".[63] Ibrahim al-Nakha'i says: "It is Sunnah to hasten the *iftar*".[64]

With what should one break the fast?

It is Sunnah to break the fast with dates. Salman ibn 'Amir reported that the Prophet ﷺ said: "When one of you is fasting, he should break his fast with dates; but if he cannot get any, then (he should break his fast) with water, for water is purifying".[65] Anas ibn Malik narrated: "The Apostle of Allah ﷺ used to break his fast before praying with some fresh dates; but if there were no fresh dates, he had a few dry dates, and

---

60 . Abu Dawud, *k. al-sawm, b. ma yustahabbu min ta'jil al-fitr;* Ibn Majah, *k. al-siyam, b. ma ja'a fi ta'jil al-iftar.*
61 Muslim, *k. al-siyam, b.waqt inqida' al-sawm* ...
62 Muslim, *k. al-siyam, b. fadl al-suhur.*
63 Abu Hanifah, *K. al-athar* 71.
64 Ibn Abi Shaybah, *al-Musannaf*, vi. 127.
65 Abu Dawud, *k. al-sawm, b. ma yuftiru 'alayhi;* Ibn Majah, *k. al-siyam, b. ma ja'a 'ala ma yustahabbu al-fitr.*

if there were no dry dates, he took some mouthfuls of water".⁶⁶

READING THE QUR'AN

It is strongly recommended that one recites the Qur'an as much as possible while fasting and especially during the month of Ramadan; this is because the month of Ramadan bears very strong relations with the Qur'an. 'Abdullah ibn 'Abbas narrates: "The Prophet ﷺ was the most generous amongst the people, and he used to be more so during the month of Ramadan when Jibril visited him, and Jibril used to meet him on every night of Ramadan until the end of the month. The Prophet used to recite the Holy Qur'an to Jibril, and when Jibril met him, he used to be more generous than a fast wind (which causes rain and welfare).⁶⁷

DU'A'

It is recommended that one makes *du'a'* (supplications) while fasting and also at the time of breaking the fast. 'Abdullah ibn 'Amr ibn al-'As narrated that the Prophet ﷺ said: "The fasting person has a supplication at the time of breaking the fast which will not be rejected".⁶⁸

Marwan ibn Salim al-Muqaffa' said: "I saw Ibn 'Umar holding his beard with his hand and cutting what exceeded a handful of it. He (Ibn 'Umar) said that the Prophet ﷺ when he broke his fast said:

ذَهَبَ الظَّمَأُ وَابْتَلَّتِ الْعُرُوقُ وَثَبَتَ الْأَجْرُ إِنْ شَاءَ اللهُ تَعَالَى

"Thirst has gone, the arteries are moist, and the reward is sure, if Allah wills".⁶⁹

Mu'adh ibn Zuhrah narrates: "The Prophet of Allah ﷺ used to say when he broke his fast:

اللَّهُمَّ لَكَ صُمْتُ وَعَلَى رِزْقِكَ أَفْطَرْتُ

'O Allah, for You I have fasted, and with Your provision I have broken my fast'".⁷⁰

---

66 Abu Dawud, *k. alsawm, b. ma yuftiru 'alayhi*; al-Tirmidhi, *k. al-sawm, b. ma ja'a ma yustahabbu al-fitr*.
67 al-Bukhari, *k. al-sawm, b. ajwad ma kana al-nabi* ..; Muslim, *k. alfada'l, b. kan al-nabi*....
68 Ibn Majah, *k. al-siyam, b. fi al-sa'im la turraddu da'watuhu*.
69 Abu Dawud, *k. al-sawm, b. al-qawl 'inda al-iftar*.
70 Ibid.

REFRAINING FROM SINS AND VAIN PURSUITS

The fasting person should control his tongue and refrain from any sinful or useless words and actions. Abu Hurayrah narrated that the Messenger of Allah ﷺ said: "Fasting is a shield. So, the person observing the fast should not use obscene language, and should not behave foolishly and impudently, and if somebody fights with him or abuses him, he should say to him: 'I am fasting, 'I am fasting".[71] Abu Hurayrah also narrated that the Prophet ﷺ said: "Whoever does not give up forged speech and evil actions, Allah is not in need of him leaving his food and drink".[72] And that the Prophet ﷺ said: "When it is the day of fasting for any of you, he should neither use obscene language nor do any act of ignorance. And if anyone slanders him or quarrels with him, he should say: "I am fasting".[73]

Abu Salih al-Hanafi narrates from his brother Talq ibn Qays that Abu Dharr said: "When you fast refrain as much as you can ". Abu Salih says: "Whenever Talq fasted, he would not leave his house except for a prayer".[74] Jabir says: "When you fast, then your ears, your eyes and your tongue also should fast from lying and sin, leave hurting the servant, there should be calmness and seriousness upon you on the day of your fasting, and do not make the day of not fasting and the day of fasting the same".[75] It has been narrated from 'Umar and 'Ali that: "Fasting does not mean abstaining from eating and drinking: rather fasting means abstaining from lying, and false and useless things".[76]

---

71 al-Bukhari, *k. al-sawm, b. hal yaqulu inna sa'im idha shutima;* Muslim, *k. al-siyam, b. fadl al-siyam.*
72 al- Bukhalri. *K. al-sawm, b. man lam yada' qawl al-zur.*
73 Ibn Majah, *k. al-siyam, b. ma ja'a fi al- ghibati wa al-rafath li al- sa'im.*
74 Ibn Abi Shaybah, al-Musannaf, vi. 98-99.
75 Ibid., vi. 100.
76 Ibid., vi. 101.

Chapter 4
TYPES OF FASTING

There are five types of fasting, they are:
1. Fasting during the month of Ramadan
2. *Qada'* and *kaffarah;*
3. Fasting of a specific vow
4. Fasting of a nonspecific vow
5. *Nafl* fasting.

I will discuss the fasting of the month of Ramadan, then I will discuss *nafl* fasting. Other types of fasting will be explained in their relevant places.

THE FASTING OF RAMADAN

Ramadan, the 9th month of Islamic calendar, has been chosen by Allah for fasting. The Qur'an, Sunnah and *Ijma* (consensus) of the *ummah* all affirm the obligatory nature of fasting during the month of Ramadan.

Allah, Exalted is He, says: *"O you who have believed, decreed upon you is fasting as it was decreed upon those before you that you may become righteous -[Fasting For] a limited number of days. So whoever among you is ill or on a journey [during them] then an equal number of days [are to be made up]. And upon those who are able [to fast, but with hardship] - a ransom [as a substitute] of feeding a poor person [each day]. And whoever volunteers excess- it is better for him. But to fast is best for you, if you only knew. The month of Ramadan [is that] in which was revealed the Qur'an, a guidance for the people and clear proofs of guidance and criterion. So whoever sights [the new moon of] the month, let him fast it; and whoever is ill or on a journey – then an equal number of other days. Allah intends for you ease and does not intend for you hardship and [wants] for you to complete the period and to glorify Allah for that [to] which he Has guided you; and perhaps you will be grateful*".⁷⁷

'Abdullah ibn 'Umar reported that the Prophet ﷺ said: "Islam is built on five things: bearing witness that there is no god but Allah and that Muhammad is the Messenger of Allah, establishing the prayer, giving the zakah, fasting the month of Ramadan, and the *hajj* (the pilgrimage to Makkah) of the House".⁷⁸

Talhah ibn Ubaydullah narrated: "A Bedouin with unkempt hair came to the Messenger of Allah ﷺ and said: 'O Messenger of Allah, inform me of what Allah has made obligatory on me as regards praying'. He replied: 'Five *salahs,* unless you do others voluntarily'. He asked the Prophet to inform him about fasting, and he said: 'The fast of Ramadan, unless you do others voluntarily'. Then he asked him about charity and the Messenger of Allah informed him ... The Bedouin then said: 'By the One who has honoured you, I shall not add anything to it, nor shall I be deficient in what Allah has ordered me to do'. The Messenger of Allah ﷺ then said: 'He will enter Paradise if he is true to this'."⁷⁹

The *ummah* has consensus on the obligatory nature of the fasting during Ramadan. It is a pillar of Islam; no one denies it except an unbeliever.⁸⁰

When was fasting made obligatory?

Fasting during the month of Ramadan was made obligatory in the month of Sha'ban in the 2nd year of the *hijrah*. The Prophet fasted for nine Ramadans. 'A'ishah narrated that "People used to fast on 'Ashura' (the 10th day of the month *Muharram*) before the fasting of Ramadan was made obligatory. And on that day the *Ka'bah* used to be covered with a cover. When Allah made fasting during the month of Ramadan compulsory, the Messenger of Allah ﷺ said: 'Whoever wishes to fast (on the day of 'Ashura') may do so; and whoever wishes to leave it can do so'."⁸¹ 'Abdullah ibn 'Umar reported that (the Arabs of) pre-Islamic days used to observe the fast on the day of 'Ashura' and the Messenger of Allah ﷺ observed it and the Muslims too (observed it) before fasting during Ramadan became obligatory. But when it became obligatory,

---

77 *Al-Baqarah* 183-185.
78 Al-Bukhari. *K. al-iman, b. du'a'ukum imanukum;* Muslim, *k. al-iman, b. bayan arkan al-islam wa da'a'imihi al-'izam.*
79 al- Bukhari, *k. iman, b. al-zakah min al-islam.*
80 Al-Kasani, *Bada'I al-sana'I,* ii. 550.
81 Abu Dawud, *k. al-siyam, b. sawm yawm 'ashura'.*

the Messenger of Allah ﷺ said: 'Ashura' is one of the days of Allah, so he who wishes should observe the fast and he who wishes otherwise should abandon it'."[82]

Ibn al-Qayyim says: "Since to liberate man from the clutches of sensuality is an extremely difficult task and it takes a lot of time, the command of the obligation of fasting was not revealed until such time after the migration when it had become clear that the creed of monotheism and the duty of *salah* had sunk deep into them and they had become thoroughly oriented to the injuctions of the Qur'an. The command of fasting, was, thus, revealed in the second year of migration and the Prophet kept the fasts of Ramadan for nine years before he departed from the world".[83]

THE VIRTUES OF THE MONTH OF RAMADAN

The month of Ramadan has special virtue. There are many *ahadith* confirming the virtues of this month, some of which includes:

Abu Hurayrah narrated that the Messenger of Allah ﷺ said: "When Ramadan begins, the gates of Paradise are opened and the gates of Hell are closed and the devils are chained".[84]

One of the great virtues of this month is that after fasting the whole month, one's sins are forgiven. Abu Hurayrah narrates: "The Prophet ﷺ said: 'Whoever established prayers on the night of *Qadr* out of sincere faith, and hoping for a reward from Allah, then all his previous sins will be forgiven'."[85]

The Prophet ﷺ used to be more active during the month of Ramadan. 'Abdullah ibn 'Abbas narrates: "The Prophet was the most generous amongst the people, and he used to be more so during the month of Ramadan when Jibril visited him, and Jibril used to meet him on every night of Ramadan until the end of the month. The Prophet used to recite the Holy Qur'an to Jibril, and when Jibril met him, he used to be more generous than a fast wind (which causes rain and welfare)".[86]

---

82 Muslim, *k. al-siyam, b. sawm yawm 'ashura'*.
83 Ibn al-Qayyim, *Zad al-ma'ad*, ii. 30.
84 Al-Bukhari, *k. al-sawm, b. hal yuqalu ramadan;* Muslim, *k. al-siyam, b. fadl shahr ramadan.*
85 Al-Bukhari, *k. al-iman, b. sawm ramadan ihtisaban min al-iman;* Muslim, *k. salat al-musafirin, b. al-targhib fi qiyam ramadan.*
86 Al-Bukhari, *k. al-sawm, b. ajwad ma kana al-nabi* ...; Muslim, *k. al-fada'il, b.*

The following hadith makes the reward of fasting unique compared to all other acts of worship. Abu Hurayrah narrated that the Prophet ﷺ said: "Allah said: 'all the deeds of Adam's sons (people) are for them, except fasting which is for Me, and I will give the reward for it'. Fasting is a shield or protection from the fire and from committing sins. If one of you is fasting, he should avoid obscene language and quarrelling, and if somebody should fight or quarrel with him, he should say: 'I am fasting'. By Him in Whose Hands my soul is, the unpleasant smell coming out from the mouth of a fasting person is better in the sight of Allah than the smell of musk. There are two pleasures for the fasting person, one at the time when he will meet his Lord; then he will be pleased because of his fasting'."[87]

The sin of not fasting during Ramadan

There are many warnings for those who do not fast during the month of Ramadan. For example: 'Abdullah ibn Abbas reported that the Prophet ﷺ said: "The ties of Islam and the foundations of religion are three, and whoever leaves one of them becomes an unbeliever, and his blood becomes lawful: testifying that there is no god but Allah, the obligatory *salahs*, and the fast of Ramadan".[88]

Abu Hurayrah reported that the Messenger of Allah ﷺ said: "Whoever breaks his fast during Ramadan without having one of the excuses that Allah will excuse him for, then even a perpetual fast, if he were to fast it, will not make up for that day".[89]

The wisdom behind fixing days for fasting

Shah Waliullah writes: "If the right to exercise one's own judgement in fasting is conceded it will open the door of evasion, the path of sanctioning what is prohibited will be obstructed and this foremost event of obeisance in Islam will fall into negligence ... It was also necessary to determine its period and duration so that no room would be left for excess or slackness. But for it, some people would have been fruitless

---

    kan al-nabi ...
87 Al-Bukhari, *k. al-sawm, b. hal yaqulu inna sa'im idha shutima*; Muslim, *k. al-siyam, b. fadl al-siyam.*
88 Abu Ya'la, *al-Musnad* 2349.
89 Abu Dawud, *k. al-sawm, b. al-taghliz fi man aftara 'amdan;* Ibn Majah, *k. al-siyam, b. ma ja'a fi kaffarati man aftara yawman min ramadan.*

while others would have carried it so far as to inflict upon themselves excessive hardship. In truth, fasting is a remedy to counteract the effects of the poison of sensuality and, therefore, it is essential that it should be administered in the right quantity".[90]

ON WHOM THE FASTING IS OBLIGATORY

Fasting during the month of Ramadan is obligatory upon Muslims who are sane and have reached puberty. 'Ali ibn Abi Talib related that the Messenger of Allah ﷺ said: "The pen is raised for three [meaning that there is no obligation upon three categories of individuals] namely those who are sleeping until they waken, the child until it becomes an adult and the insane until they become sane".[91]

If a child becomes of age or a *kafir* (non-Muslim) becomes a Muslim during Ramadan, then that individual must abstain from eating, drinking or sexual intercourse for the rest of that day and then carry on fasting the days following this but they do not make up the days missed.[92]

If one faints during Ramadan then one is not required to make up the day on which one fainted, but one does have to make up the following missed days if any.[93] This is on condition that the person has not done anything to break the fast. If the person remains unconscious the next day, their intention to fast the day on which they fainted is no longer valid.

Although fasting is not obligatory on one who is insane, if such a person recovers his sanity during a Ramadan then he is obliged to fast the remaining days of the month and make up any days in that month before he recovered his senses.[94]

The fasting of children

Fasting is not compulsory for children through their guardians are commanded to instil love for and a habit of fasting in them from an early age. Rubayyi' bint Mu'awwidh narrated: "The Prophet ﷺ sent a messenger to the village of the Ansar in the morning of the day of 'Ashura' to announce: 'Whoever has eaten something should not eat

---

90   Al-Dihlawi, *Hujjatullah al-balighah*, ii. 75-76.
91   Abu Dawud, *k. al-hudud, b. fi al-majnun yassriq*; al-Tirmidhi, *k. al-hudud, b. ma ja'a fi man la yajibu 'alayh al-hadd.*
92   Al-Quduri, al-Mukhtasar 195.
93   Ibid.
94   ibid

but complete the fast, and whoever is observing the fast should complete it'." She further said: "Since then we used to fast on that day regularly and also make our children fast. We used to make toys of wool for the boys and if anyone of them cried he was given those toys until it was the time of breaking the fast".[95]

Ibn Sirin says: "The child should be commanded to perform *salah* when he recognizes his right hand from his left and fasting when he can do it".[96] The same has been narrated from al-Zuhri, Qatadah and 'Urwah ibn al-Zubayr.[97]

Women in a state of menstruation

Women in a state of menstruation or postnatal bleeding are not allowed to fast. Abu Sa'id reported that the Prophet ﷺ said: "Isn't it true that a woman does not pray and does not fast on menstruating? And that is the defect (a loss) on her religion".[98]

Nevertheless the fasting is obligatory on those women, and they have to complete the number of days of fasting later.

It is reported that Mu'adhah al-'Adawiyyah asked 'Aishah: "Why is it that a woman in a state menstruation does the *qada'* of fasting, not the *qada'* of *salah*".[99] There is no harm if the women delay the *qada'* for a reason. 'Aishah narrated: "Sometimes I missed some days of Ramadan, but could not fast in lieu of them except in the month of Sha'ban". Yahya ibn Sa'id, a sub-narrator, says: "She used to be busy serving the Prophet ﷺ".[100]

If a woman begins her menstruation or has post-natal bleeding while fasting, she breaks her fast and makes it up when she becomes pure again. Similarly, if a woman becomes pure after dawn, she is not allowed to fast that day neither for Ramadan not for any voluntary fast.[101]

---

95 Al-Bukhari, *k. al-sawm, b. sawm al-sibyan*; Muslim, *k. al-siyam, b. an ahada fi 'ashura' fatyakuffa baqiyyata yawmihi*.
96 'Abd al-Razzaq, *al-Musannaf*, iv. 153.
97 Ibid.
98 Al-Bukhari, *k. al-hayd, b. tark al-ha'id al-sawm*; Muslim, *k. al-iman, b. bayin nuqsan al-iman bi naqs al-ta'at*.
99 Muslim, *k. al-hayd, b. wujub qada' al-sawm 'ala al-ha'id*.
100 Al-Bukhari, *k. al-sawm, b. mata yaqdi qada'a ramadan*; Muslim, *k. al-siyam, d. qada' ramadan fi sha'ban*.
101 Al-Kasani, Bada'I *al-sana'I*. ii. 596-7,

The invalid and the traveller

As for those who are ill or travelling, it is permitted for them not to fast during the month of Ramadan for the duration of their illness or travel. The Qur'an states: *"So whoever sights [the new moon of] the month, let him fast it; and whoever is ill or on a journey – then an equal number of other days. Allah intends for you ease and does not intend for you hardship and [wants] for you to complete the period and to glorify Allah for that [to] which He has guided you; and perhaps you will be grateful"*.[102] Abu al-Darda' narrated: "We set out with Allah's Messenger on one of his journeys on a very hot day. It was so hot that one had to put ones hand over ones head because of the severity of the heat. None of us was fasting except the Prophet ﷺ and Ibn Rawahah".[103]

Nevertheless, if a sick person fasts during his illness and a traveller fasts during his journey, this is allowed. 'A'ishah narrates: "Hamzah ibn 'Amr al-Aslami asked the Prophet: 'Should I fast while travelling?' The Prophet replied: 'You may fast if you wish, and you may not fast if you wish'."[104] Anas ibn Malik narrated: "We were travelling with the Prophet ﷺ while some of us were fasting, and some of us did not fast".[105] Tawus narrated that Ibn 'Abbas said: "The Messenger of Allah ﷺ set out from Madinah to Makkah and he fasted until he reached 'Usfan, where he asked for water and raised his hand to let the people see him, and then broke the fast, and did not fast after that until he reached Makkah, and that happened during Ramadan".[106]

Ibn 'Abbas used to say: "Allah's Messenger ﷺ (sometimes) fasted and (sometimes) did not fast during journeys so whoever wished to fast could fast, and whoever wished not to fast, could do so".[107] Abu Sa'id al-Khudri reported: "We went out on an expedition with Allah's Mes-

---

102 Al-Baqarah 185.
103 Al-Bukhari, *k. al-sawm b. idha sama ayyaman min ramadan*. Al-Bukhari, *k. al-sawm, b. al-sawm fi al-safar wa al-iftar*; Muslim, *k. al-siyam, b. al-takhyir fi al-sawm wa al-fitr fi al-safar*.
104 Al-Bukhari, *k. al-sawm, b. al-sawm fi al-safar wa al-iftar*; Muslim, *k. al-siyam, b. al-takhyir fi al-sawm wa al-fitr fi al-safar*.
105 Al-Bukhari, *k. al—jihad, b. fadl al-khidmah fi al-al-ghazw*, Muslim, *k. al-siyam, b. ajr al-muftar fi al-safar idha tawalla al-'amal*.
106 Al-Bukhari, *k. al-sawm, b. man aftara fi al-safar li yarahu al-nas*; Muslim, *k. al-siyam, b. jawaz al-sawm wa al-fitr fi shahr ramadan li al-musafir*.
107 Al-Bukhari, *k. al-sawm, b. man aftara fi al-safar li yarahu al-nas*; Muslim, *k. al-siyam, b. jawaz al-sawm wa al-fitr fi shahr ramadan li al-musafir*.

senger 🕊 on the 16th of Ramadan. Some of us fasted and some of us broke the fast. But neither the observer of the fast found fault with the one who observed it".[108]

However, if the fasting affects them, then it is better not to fast, Ibn 'Abbas narrated: "The Messenger of Allah 🕊 set out for Makkah during Ramadan and he fasted, and when he reached Al-Kadid, he broke his fast and the people with him broke their fast too". Al-Bukhari said: "Al-Kadid is a place of water between 'Usfan and Qudayd".[109] Jabir ibn 'Abdullah narrates an incident while the Messenger of Allah 🕊 was on a journey and saw a crowd of people shading a man. Upon seeing this, the Prophet 🕊 asked: "What is the matter?" They said: "He (the man) is fasting". The Prophet said: "It is not righteousness that you fast on a journey".[110] Jabir ibn 'Abdullah also reported that: "The Messenger of Allah 🕊 went out to Makkah during Ramadan in the year of Victory, and he and the people fasted until he came to Kura' al-Ghumaym. He then called for a cup of water which he raised until the people saw it, and then he drank. He was told afterwards that some people had continued to fast, and he said: 'These people are the disobedient ones; they are the disobedient ones'."[111]

However, if the journey is comfortable and one feels no difficulty then one should fast. Salamah ibn al-Muhabbaq al-Hudhali narrated: "The Apostle of Allah 🕊 said: 'If anyone has a riding beast which carries him to where he can get sufficient food, he should keep the fast of Ramadan wherever he is when it comes'."[112]

When the sick person has been cured and the traveller has returned home, then they must fast the numbers of the day which they have missed.[113]

If the sick person or traveller dies and they die in this state of being ill or travelling, then the obligation of having to make up their fast is removed and therefore no *kaffarah* is required to be paid by their inheritors.[114]

---

108   Muslim, *k. al-siyam, b. jawaz al-sawm wa al-fitr fi shahr ramadan li al-musafir*.
109   Al-Bukhari, *k. al-sawm, b. idha sama ayyaman fi ramadan thumma safar*.
110   Al-Bukhari, *k. al-sawm, b. qawl al-nabi sallallahu 'alayhi wa sallam liman onzilah 'alayah;* Muslim, *k. al-siyam, b. jawaz al-sawm wa al-fitr fi shahr ramadan li al-musafir*.
111   Muslim, *k. al-siyam, b. jawaz al-sawm wa al-fitr fi shahr ramadan li al-musafir*.
112   Abu Dawud, *k. al-sawm, b. man ikhtara al-siyam*.
113   Al-Quduri, *al-Mukhtasar 192*.
114   Ibid, 193.

If the sick person recovers or the traveller becomes resident, and then they die, the obligation of making up for the missed days of fasting in accordance with the number of days they were healthy or resident prior to their death remains.[115] In such cases *kaffarah* is required to be paid by their inheritors.

If a traveller arrives at his destination or the menstruating woman becomes pure at some moment during the day, then out of respect for the month, they should abstain from eating, drinking or intercourse for the rest of that day.[116]

Those physically unable to fast

As for the elderly and the sick that are unable to fast and there is no hope of their recovery, then they are excused from fasting. Instead, they should feed a poor person half a *sa'* of wheat or a *sa'* of dates or barley for each day of the fast.[117] When Anas ibn Malik reached old age and was unable to fast, he commanded that the poor be fed; so they were fed bread and meat until they were full.[118]

If a pregnant woman or beast feeding mother fear for the wellbeing of their children or themselves, then they may break their fast and make it up, but they are not required to pay any compensation.[119] Anas ibn Malik, a man from the *Banu* (clan) of 'Abdullah ibn Ka'b brethren of *Banu* Qushayr (not Anas ibn Malik, the well-known Companion), said: "A contingent from the cavalry of the Apostle of Allah ﷺ raided us, I reached", or (he said,) "I went to the Apostle of Allah ﷺ who was taking his meals. He said: 'Sit down, and take some from this meal of ours'. I said: 'I am fasting,' he said: 'Sit down. I shall tell you about prayer and fasting. Allah has lifted (the obligation) of half the prayer for a traveller, and (that of) fasting for the traveller, and from the woman who is suckling an infant or the woman who is pregnant'. I swear by Allah, he mentioned both (i.e. suckling and pregnant women) or one of them. I deeply regretted not eating from the meal of the Apostle of Allah ﷺ'."[120] Imam

---

115 Ibid.
116 Al-Kasani, Bada'I al-sana'I , ii. 596-7.
117 Al-Quduri, *al-Mukhtasar* 194; ibid., ii. 616.
118 Al-Bukhari, *k. al-tafsir, b. ayyaman ma'dudat ....*
119 Al-Kasani, *Bada'i al-sana'I* , ii. 614-5.
120 Abu Dawud, *k. al-sawm, b. ikhtiyar al-fitr; al-Tirmidhi, k. al-sawm, b. ma ja'a fi al-rukhsah fi al-iftar li al-hubla wa al-murdi; al-Nasa'I, k. al-siyam, b. wad'*

al-Tirmidhi after narrating this hadith said: "The people of knowledge follow this hadith whereby the woman who is sucking an infant and the woman who is pregnant, when they fear for the wellbeing of their children, are allowed not to fast, but later they will do *qada*".

Whoever dies while still under the obligation of making up missed fasts of Ramadan and he has given instructions in this regard, in his testament or before his death, then his executor on his behalf feeds a destitute person half a *sa'* of wheat or a *sa'* of dates or barley for each day not fasted.[121] 'Abdullah ibn 'Umar narrated that the Prophet ﷺ said: "For the one who has died whist having the obligation of fasting a month, one poor person should be fed, on his behalf, (in compensation) for every day (of fast due.)"[122] This is also the opinion of Ibrahim al-Nakha'i, Malik, Sufyan al-Thawi and Shafi'i.[123]

NAFL FAST

Nafl fast include all Sunnah, recommended and voluntary fasting. Fasting is encouraged in Islam and people are advised to do voluntary fasts beside the fasting of Ramadan. 'Abdullah ibn Shaqiq reported: "I said to 'Aishah: 'Did the Apostle of Allah ﷺ observe the fast for a full month besides Ramadan?' She said: 'I do not know of any month in which he fasted throughout, but that of the month of Ramadan, and I do not know a month in which he did not fast at all, until he ran the course of his life'."[124] 'Abdullah ibn 'Abbas reported: "The Messenger of Allah ﷺ did not fast throughout any month except Ramadan. And when he observed the fast, he fasted so continousely that one would say that he would not break them and when he abandoned (fasting), he anbandoned so continuously that one would say: 'By Allah, perhaps he would never fast'."[125]

There are certain voluntary fasts which are recommended by the Prophet ﷺ. These are mentioned below:

---

al-siyam an al-hubla wa al-murdi; Ibn Majah, k. al-siyam, b. ma ja'a fi al-iftar li al-hamid wa al-murdi'.

121 Al-Quduri, *al-Mukhtar* 194.
122 Al-Tirmidhi, *k. al-sawm, b. ma ja'a min al-kaffarah.*
123 Al-Baghawi, *Sharh al-sunnah*, iii. 510.
124 Muslim, *k. al-siyam, b. siyam al-nabi sallallahu 'alayhi wa sallam fi ghayr ramadan.*
125 Al- Bukhari, *k. al-sawm, b. ma yudhkaru min sawm al-nabi sallallahu 'alayhi wa sallam wa iftarih;* Muslim, *k. al-siyam, b. siyam al-nabi sallallahu 'alayhi wa sallam fi ghayr ramadan.*

The six days of Shawwal

Abu Ayyub al-Ansari reported Allah's Messenger ﷺ said: "For him who observed the fast of Ramadan and then followed it with six days of fasting during the month of *Shawwal*, it is as if he fasted perpetually".[126]

It is perhaps better not to fast continuously during the few days after *'id* in order to avoid it seeming to extend Ramadan, and to distinguish *fard* from Sunnah.[127]

The Day of 'Arafah

It is recommended that one fasts on the Day of 'Arafah[128] (9th Dhu al-hijjah.)

Abu Qatadah narrated that the Messenger of Allah ﷺ said: "Fasting on the Day of 'Arafah removes the sins of two years: the previous year and the coming year".[129]

However, it is disliked for those performing *hajj* to fast on the Day of 'Arafah. 'Ikrimah said: "We were with Abu Hurayrah in his house when he narrated on us: "The Apostle of Allah ﷺ prohibited fasting on the Day of 'Arafah at 'Arafah'.[130] Umm al-Fadl bint al-Harith narrated: "While the people were with me on the Day of 'Arafah they differed as to whether the Prophet was fasting or not; some said that he was fasting while others said that he was not fasting. So, I sent to him a bowl full of milk while he was riding over his camel and he drank it".[131] Kurayb, who was the freed slave of Ibn 'Abbas reports from Maymunah, the wife of the Apostle of Allah ﷺ that: "People had doubt about the fasting of Allah's Messenger on the day of 'Arafah. Maymunah sent him a cup of milk and he was halting at a place and he drank it and the people saw him".[132]

---

126 Muslim, *k. al-siyam, b. istihbab sawm sittati ayyam min shawwal.*
127 Al-Samarqandi, *Tuhfat al-fuqaha'* 163; al-Kasani, *Bada'i al-sana'i.* ii 562.
128 'Arafah is a pilgrimage site in Makkah, Staying there on the 9th of *Dhu al-hijjah is the most important pillar of the hajj.*
129 Muslim, *k. al-siyam, b. istihbab thalathati ayyam min kulli shahr...*
130 Abu Dawud, *k. al-sawm, b. fi sawm yawm 'Arafah bi 'Arafah;* al-Nasa'i, *k. al haj b. al-nahy 'an sawm yawm 'Arafah.*
131 Al-Bukhari, k. *al-sawm, b. sawm yawm 'Arafah;* Muslim, *k. al-siyam, b.istihbab al-fitr li al-hajj yawm 'Arafah.*
132 Muslim, *k. al-siyam, b. istihbab al-fitr li al-hajj yawm 'Arafah.*

'Ashura'

'Ashura' means the 10th of Muharram. The Prophet ﷺ used to fast that day, and he said the year he died that if he lived the next year then he would fast one day before it or one day after it. The reason being to avoid similarity with the Jews who fasted the 10th only. Since then the established Sunnah is to fast on the 9th and 10th or 10th and 11th of Muharram.

'Abdullah ibn 'Umar said that: "The Arabs of pre-Islamic days observed the fast on the Day of 'Ashura' and the Messenger of Allah ﷺ observed it and so did the Muslims. This was before fasting during Ramadan became obligatory. When fasting during Ramadan became obligatory. When fasting during Ramadan became obligatory, the Messenger of Allah ﷺ said: 'Ashura' is one of the Days of Allah, so he who wishes should observe the fast and he who wishes otherwise should abandon it'."[133]

Ibn 'Abbas said: "When the Messenger of Allah ﷺ fasted on the Day of 'Ashura' and commanded that it should be observed as a fast, they (his Companions) said to him: 'Messenger of Allah, it is a day which the Jews and Christians hold in high esteem'. Thereupon, the Messenger of Allah ﷺ said: 'When the next year comes, Allah willing, we will observe the fast on the 9th'. But the Messenger of Allah ﷺ died before the advent of the next year'."[134]

Abu Qatadah narrated that the Messenger of Allah ﷺ said: "Fasting on the Day of 'Ashura'. I expect from Allah, the removal of the sins of the previous year".[135]

Fasting on Mondays and Thursdays

The Prophet ﷺ mostly kept fast on Mondays and Thursdays. Abu Hurayrah narrates: "The Prophet mostly fasted on Mondays and Thursdays. On being asked about this, the Prophet said: 'The deeds are presented (to Allah) every Monday and Thursday, then Allah forgives the sins of every Muslim except two who cut ties (with each other); it is said (about them): 'delay them'."[136] The client of Usamah ibn Zayd said that he went along with Usamah to Wadi al-Qura in pursuit of his camels. Usamah would fast on Mondays and Thursdays. His client said to him: "Why do

---

133 Muslim, *k. al-siyam, b. sawm yawm 'ashura'*.
134 Muslim, *k. al-siyam, b. ayy yawm yusamu fi 'ashura'*.
135 Muslim, *k. al-siyam, b. istihbab thalathati ayyam mun kulli shahr...*
136 Al-Tirmidhi, *k. alsawm, b. ma ja'a fi sawm al-ithanyn wa al-khamis*; Ibn Majah, *k. al-siyam, b. siyam yawm al-ithnan wa al-khamis*.

you fast on Monday and Thursday while you are an old man?" He said: "The Prophet of Allah ﷺ used to fast on Monday and Thursday. When he was asked about this, he said: "The deeds of the slaves are presented on Mondays and Thursdays"."[137] It has been narrated from a large number of Companions and Successors that they kept fast on Mondays and Thursdays. Among them are, 'Ali, 'Abdullah ibn Mas'ud, Abu Hurayrah, Usamah ibn Zayd, 'Umar ibn 'Abd al-'Aziz and Makhul.[138]

Three days of every month

It is recommended that one fasts three days in every month: namely 13th, 14th and 15th. 'Abdullah ibn Mas'ud narrated: "The Apostle of Allah ﷺ used to fast three days every month".[139] Qatadah ibn Milhan al-Qaysi narrated: "The Apostle of Allah ﷺ used to command us to fast the days of the white nights (full moon): the 13th, 14th and 15th of the month. He (the Prophet ﷺ) said: "This is like keeping a perpetual fast'."[140]

Abu Qatadah reported that: "A person came to the Apostle of Allah ﷺ and said: 'How do you observe the fast?' The Messenger of Allah ﷺ felt annoyed. When 'Umar noticed his annoyance, he said: 'We are well pleased with Allah as our lord, with Islam as our Code of Life, and with Muhammad as our Prophet. We seek refuge with Allah from the anger of Allah and that of His Messenger'. 'Umar kept on repeating these words until his (the Prophet's) anger calmed down. Then 'Umar said: 'Messenger of Allah, what is the position of one who perpetually observes the fast?' Thereupon, he said: 'He neither fasted nor broke it,' or he said: 'He did not fast and he did not break it'. He ('Umar) said: 'What about him who observes the fast for two days and breaks one day'. Thereupon, he said: 'Is any one capable of doing it?' He ('Umar) said: 'What is the position of him who observes the fast for a day and breaks on the other day?' Thereupon, he (the Prophet) said: 'That is the fast of David (peace be upon him)'. He ('Umar) said; 'What about him who observes the fast one day and breaks it for two days'. Thereupon,

---

137 Abu Dawud, *k. al-siyam, b. sawm al-ithnayn wa al-khamis.*
138 Ibn Abi Shaybah, *al-Musanannaf,* vi. 190-193.
139 Abu Dawud, *k. al-sawm, b. fi sawm al-thalath min kulli shahr,* al-Tirmidhi, *k. al-sawm, b. ma ja'a fi sawm yawm al-jumu'ah;* al-Nasa'I, *k. al-siyam, b. sawm al-nabi sallallahu 'alayhi wa sallam.*
140 Abu-Dawud, *k. al-sawm, b. fi sawm al-thalath min kulli shahr,* Ibn Majah, *k. al-siyam, b. ma ja'a fi siyam thalathat ayyam min kulli shahr.*

he (the Messenger of Allah) said: 'I wish I were given the strength to observe that'. Thereafter, he said: 'The observance of three days fast every month and that of Ramadan every year is perpetual fasting, I seek from Allah that fasting on the Day of 'Arafah may atone for the sins of the preceding and coming years. And I seek from Allah that fasting on the Day of Ashura may atone for the sins of the preceding year'."[141]

Fasting on alternate days

'Abdullah ibn 'Amr ibn al-'As narrates: "The Messenger of Allah ﷺ said to me: 'O 'Abdullah! Have I not been informed that you fast during the day and offer prayers all the night?" 'Abdullah replied: 'Yes, O Messenger of Allah'. The Prophet said: 'Don't do that, fast for a few days and then give it up for a few days, offer prayers and also sleep at night, as your body has a right on you, and your wife has a right on you, and your guest has a right on you. And it is sufficient for you to fast three days in a month, as the reward of a good deed is multiplied ten times, so it will be like fasting throughout the year'. I insisted (on fasting) and so I was given a hard instruction. I said: 'O Allah's Apostle! I have power'. The Prophet said: 'Fast like the fasting of the Prophet David and do not fast more than that'. I said: 'How was the fasting of the Prophet of Allah, David?' He said: 'Half of the year', (i.e. he used to fast on every alternate day)'." It is reported that when 'Abdullah became old, he used to say: "It would have been better for me if I had accepted the permission of the Prophet which he gave me (to fast only three days a month)".[142]

When voluntary fasting becomes compulsory

Whoever begins a voluntary fast but then invalidates it, must make up for it. Details about this will be given later in the chapter.

---

141 Muslim, *k. al-siyam, b. istihbab thalathat ayyam min kulli shahr.*
142 Al-Bukhari, *k. al-sawm, b. haqq al-jism fi al-sawm;* Muslim, *k. al-siyam, b. al-nahy 'an sawm al-dahr.*

Chapter 5
DAYS WHEN FASTING IS FORBIDDEN OR DISLIKED

THERE ARE CERTAIN days when fasting is either forbidden or disliked.

FORBIDDEN DAYS
There are five days during the year when fasting is forbidden namely, the Day of 'Id *al-fitr*, the Day of *'Id al-adha*, and the three days of tashriq (11th, 12th and 13th Dhl al-hijjah). Abu 'Ubayd says: "I attended *'Id* Prayer with 'Umar ibn al-Khattab; he started the prayer before the *khutbah* and said: 'The Messenger of Allah ﷺ forbade fasting of these two days: the day of *'Id al-fitr,* and the Day of Sacrifice (*'Id al-adha*). As for 'Id al-fitr, that is the day when you have to eat from your sacrifice'."[143] Qaza'ah related: "I heard from Abu Sa'id a hadith which impressed me, and I said to him: 'Did you hear it from the Messenger of Allah ﷺ?' Thereupon, he said: "(Is it possible) that (I should) say about the Messenger of Allah ﷺ that which I have not heard? I heard him saying: 'It is not proper to fast on two days, Day of *fitr* (at the end) of Ramadan, and the Day of Sacrifice'."[144]

Abu Hurayrah narrated that the Messenger of Allah ﷺ said: "The days of Mina (10th, 11th, 12th, and 13th) are the days of eating and drinking".[145] Nubayshah al-Hudhali reported Allah's Messenger ﷺ as saying: "The days of *tashriq* are days of eating and drinking".[146] Ibn Ka'b ibn Malik reported on the authority of his father that the Messenger of Allah ﷺ sent him and Aws ibn Hadathan during the days of *tashriq* to make this announcement: "None but the believer would be admitted into Paradise, and the

---

143 Al- Bukhari, *k. al-sawm, yawm al-fitr;* Muslim, *k. al-siyam, b. al-nahy 'an sawm yawm al-fitr wa yawm al-adha.*
144 Ibid.
145 Muslim, *k. al-siyam, b. sawm ayyam al-tashriq.*
146 Muslim, *k. al-siyam, b. tahrim sawm ayyam al-tashriq.*

days of Mina are the days meant for eating and drinking".[147]

DISLIKED DAYS
There are certain days when fasting is disliked.

Day of doubt
Fasting is disliked on the day of doubt; the details of which have been mentioned earlier.

Friday
Fasting on Friday alone is disliked, but if one fasts one day before or after it as well, then there is no harm. 'Abdullah ibn 'Amr reported that the Messenger of Allah entered the room of Juwayriyah bint al-Harith while she was fasting on a Friday. He asked her: "Did you fast yesterday?" She answered, "No". He said: "Do you plan to fast tomorrow?" She answered, "No". Therefore he said: "Then break your fast".[148]

Muhammad ibn 'abbad ibn Ja'far reported: "I asked Jabir ibn 'Abdullah while he was circumambulating the House (Ka'bah) whether the Messenger of Allah ﷺ had forbidden fasting on Friday, whereupon he said: 'Yes, by the Lord of His House'."[149] Abu Hurayrah reported the Apostle of Allah ﷺ said: "None among you should observe the fast on Friday, but only that he observes the fast before it and after it".[150]

Saturday
It is also disliked to fast on a Saturday alone. 'Abdullah ibn Busr related from his sister al-Samma' that the Messenger of Allah ﷺ said: "Do not fast on Saturdays unless it is an obligatory fast. [You should not fast] even if you do not find anything [to eat] save some grape peelings or a branch of a tree to chew on".[151] Umm Salamah narrates: "The Prophet

---

147 Ibid.
148 Al-Bukhari, *k. al-sawm, b. sawm yawm al-jumu'ah*.
149 Al-Bukhari, *k. al-sawm, b. sawm yawm al-jumu'ah*; Muslim, *k. al-siyam, b. karahiyat sawm yawm al-jumu'ah*.
150 Al-Bukhari, *k. al-sawm, b. sawm yawm al-jumu'ah*; Muslim, *k. al-siyam, b. karahiyat sawm yawm al-jumu'ah*.
151 Abu Dawud, *k. al-sawm, b. al-nahy an yukhassa yawm al-sabt bi sawm;* al-Tirmidhi, *k. al-sawm, b. ma ja'a fi sawm yawm al-sabt;* Ibn Majah, *k. al-siyam, b. ma ja'a si siyam yawm al-sabt.*

used to fast more often on Saturdays and Sundays than on the other days. He would say: 'They are the 'Ids of the polytheists, and I love to differ from them".[152] This hadith makes it clear that if another day is added then there is no harm in fasting on Saturdays.

Wisal

Wisal means continuous fasting even after sunset; it can continue until the sunset of the next day, or even further. *Wisal* fasting is also disliked.[153] Abu Hurayrah reported that the Messenger of Allah ﷺ said: "Do not perform *al-wisal*". He said this three times and the people said to him: "But you perform *al-wisal*, O Messenger of Allah" He said: "You are not like me in that matter. I spend the night in such a state that Allah feeds me and gives me to drink. Devote yourselves to the deeds which you can perform".[154] Anas reported: "The Messenger of Allah ﷺ was observing prayer during Ramadan. I came and stood by his side. Then another man came and he stood likewise until we became a group. When the Apostle of Allah ﷺ noticed that we were behind him, he lightened the prayer. He then went to his abode and observed such (a long) prayer (the like of which) he never observed with us. When it was morning we said to him: 'Did you notice us during the night?' Upon this he said: 'Yes, it was this (realization) that led me to do that which I did'. He (the narrator) said: 'The Messenger of Allah ﷺ began to observe *wisal* fasting at the end of the month (of Ramadan), and some among his Companions began to observe *wisal* fast, whereupon the Apostle of Allah ﷺ said: 'What about such persons who observe *wisal* fasts? You are not like me. By Allah! If the month were lengthened for me, I would have observed *wisal*, so that those who act with an exaggeration would (have been obliged) to abandon their exaggeration".[155] Imam Muhammad says after narrating the above hadith of Abu Hurayrah: "We adhere to this, the *wisal* is disliked, and it is that one continues fasting for two days without eating anything at night, and that is the opinion of Abu Hanifah and the majority of scholars".[156]

---

152 Ahmed, *al-Musnad, musnad al-nisa'*.
153 Al-Samarqandi, *Tuhfat al-fuqaha'* 163.
154 Al-Bukhari, *k. al-sawm, b. ul-tankil li man aktara al-wisal;* Muslim, *k. al-siyam, b. al-nahy 'an al-wisal fi al-sawm.*
155 Muslim, *k. al-siyam, b. al-nahy 'an al-wisal fi al-sawm.*
156 Muhammad, *al-Muwatta',* 129.

The whole year

It is also disliked to fast the whole year. 'Abdullah ibn 'Amr ibn al-'As narrates that the Messenger of Allah ﷺ said: "There is no fasting for the one who continually fasts".[157] Imam al-Tirmidhi says: "A group of scholars dislike fasting every day if it includes the *'ids ('id al-Fitr, 'id al-adha)*, and the days of *tashriq*. If one breaks the fast on those days, one's action is no longer fasting the whole year".[158]

However, most scholars consider such fasting as disliked, and prefer to fast every other day like Prophet Dawud. 'Abdullah ibn 'Amr ibn al-'As reported that the Messenger of Allah ﷺ was informed that he could stand up for prayer throughout the night and observe the fast every day as long as he lived. Thereupon, the Messenger of Allah ﷺ said: "Is it you who said this? I said to him: 'Messenger of Allah, it is I who said that'. Thereupon, the Messenger of Allah ﷺ said: "You are not capable enough of doing so. Observe the fast and break it; sleep and stand for prayer, and observe the fast for three days during the month; for every good is multiplied ten times and this is like fasting forever'. I said: 'Messenger of Allah. I am capable of doing more than this. Thereupon he said: 'Fast one day and do not fast for the next two days'. I said: Messenger of Allah, 'I have the strength to do more than that'. The Prophet ﷺ said: 'Fast one day and break on the other day. That is the fasting of David ﷺ and that is the best of fast'. I said: 'I am capable of doing more than this'. Thereupon, the Messenger of Allah ﷺ said: 'There is nothing better than this'. 'Abdullah ibn 'Amr said: 'Had I accepted the three days (fasting during every month) as the Messenger of Allah ﷺ had said, it would have been dearer to me than my family and my property'.[159]

Fasting without the consent of one's husband

It is also disliked for a woman to practice *nafl* fasting while her husband is present except with his explicit consent. Abu Hurayrah reported that the Prophet ﷺ said: "A woman is not to fast (even) for one day while her husband is present except with his consent, unless it is during Ram-

---

157 Muslim, *k. al-siyam, b. al-nahy 'an sawm al-dahr*.
158 Al-Tirmidhi, *k. al-sawm, b. ma ja'a fi sawm al-dahr*.
159 Al-Bukhari, *k. al-sawm, b. haqq al-jism fi al-sawm*, Muslim, *k. al-siyam b. al-nahy 'an sam al-dahr*.

adan".[160] Abu Sa'id al-Khudri narrated: "The Apostle of Allah ﷺ forbade women from fasting without the permission of their husbands".[161]

---

160   Al-Bukhari, *k. al-nikah, b. sawm al-mar'ah bi idhn zawjiha*; Muslim, *k. al-zakah, b. ma anfaqa al-'abd min mal mawlah*; Abu Dawud, *k. al-sawm, b. al-mar'ah tasum bi ghayr idhn zawjiha*; al-Tirmidhi, *k. al-sawm, b. ma ja'a fi karahiyat sawm al-mar'ah illa bi idhn zawjiha*; Ibn Majah, *k. al-siyam, b. fi al-mar'ah tasum bi ghayr idhn zawjiha*.

161   Ibn Majah, *k. al-siyam, b. fi al-mar'ah tasum bi ghayr idhn zawjiha*.

Chapter 6
WHAT IS ALLOWED DURING FASTING

EATING AND DRINKING FOREGETFULLY

IF THE FASTING person eats, drinks or has sexual intercourse out of forgetfulness, he does not break his fast and does not have to make up [any fast] or pay any *kaffarah*.[162] Abu Hurayrah narrated that the Prophet ﷺ said: "If somebody eats or drinks forgetfully then he should complete his fast, for what he has eaten or drunk has been given to him by Allah".[163]

TASTING THE FOOD

If one tastes something (introduced into one's mouth) one does not break the fast but doing so is disliked. If a woman is obliged to chew food for her child this is also disliked. If the dust of flour or from the road or smoke enters one's throat, this does not break the fast.[164]

GETTING UP IN THE MORNING AS JUNUBI

If someone had sexual relation during the night and gets up in the morning in the state of *janabah* (a state of major impurity when *ghusl* is compulsory), it does not affect one's fasting and one can bathe during the day to become ritually clean. 'Aishah and Umm Salamah narrated: "At times the Messenger of Allah ﷺ used to get up in the morning in the state of *janabah* after having sexual relations with his wives. He would then take a bath and fast".[165]

'Aishah narrates that a person once came to the Apostle of Allah ﷺ asking him a question. The man said to the Prophet ﷺ: "Messenger of

---

162 Al-Samarqandi, *Tuhfat al-fuqaha'* 169.
163 Al-Bukhari, *k. al-sawm, b. al-sa'im idha akala aw shariba nasiyan*; Muslim, *k. al-siyam, b. akl al-nasi wa shurbuh wa jima'uhu la yuftir*.
164 Al-Samarqandi, *Tuhfat al-fuqaha'* 169; al-Kasani, *Bada'i al-sana'i*, ii. 635.
165 Al-Bukhari, *k. al-sawm, b. al-sa'im yusbihu junuban*; Muslim, *k. al-siyam, b. sihhat sawm man tala'a 'alayh al-fajr wa huwa junub*.

Allah, (the time of) prayer overtakes me as I am in a state of *janabah*; should I observe fast (in the state)?' Upon this the Messenger of Allah ﷺ said: '(At times, the time of) prayer overtakes me while I am in a state of janabah, and I observe the fast (in that very stat)'. Whereupon, he (the man) said: 'Messenger of Allah, you are not like us, Allah has pardoned all your sins, the previous ones and the later ones'. Upon this he (the Prophet) said: 'By Allah, I hope I am the most God-fearing of you, and possess the best knowledge among you of those things against which I should guard'."[166]

Abu Bakr ibn 'Abd al-Rahman ibn Harith reported: "I heard Abu Hurayrah narrating that he who is overtaken by dawn in a state of *janabah* should not observe fast. I made a mention of it to 'Abd al-Rahman ibn Harith (i.e. his father) but he denied it. 'Abd al-Rahman went and I also went along with him until we came to 'A'ishah and Umm Salamah and 'Abd al-Rahman asked them about it. Both of them said: 'At times it so happened that the Apostle of Allah ﷺ woke up in the morning in a state of *janabah*, (not because of a dream) and observed fast'. We then proceeded until we came to Marwan abd 'Abd al-Rahman made mention of it to him. Upon this Marwan said: 'I stress upon you (with an oath) that you better go to Abu Hurayrah and refute to him what is said about it'. So we came to Abu Hurayrah and 'Abd al-Rahman made mention of it to him, whereupon Abu Hurayrah said: 'Did they (the two wives of the Prophet) tell you this?' He replied: 'Yes'. Upon this Abu Hurayrah said: 'They have better knowledge'. Ibn Jurayj (one of the narrators) reported: 'I asked 'Abd al-Malik, if they (the two wives) said the statement with regard to Ramadan, whereupon he said: 'It was so, and he (the Prophet) woke up in the morning in a state of *janabah* which was not due to a wet dream and then observed the fast'."[167]

KISSING

It is allowed for husbands and wives to kiss each other during the day as long as they are sure that this will not lead to sexual relations and that they will not have an emission. 'A'ishah narrated: "The Prophet used to kiss and embrace (his wives) while he was fasting, and he had more pow-

---

166 Muslim, *k. al-siyam, sihhat sawm man tala'a 'alayh al-fajr wa huwa junab.*
167 Ibid.

er to control his desires than any of you".¹⁶⁸ 'A'ishah also narrated: "The Apostle of Allah ﷺ used to kiss during the month of Ramadan when he was fasting".¹⁶⁹ 'Umar ibn al-Khattab narrated: "I kissed my wife while I was fasting, I then said: 'Apostle of Allah, I have done a big deed; I kissed while I was fasting'. He said: 'What do you think if you rinse your mouth with water while you are fasting?'¹⁷⁰ 'A'ishah narrated that the Prophet ﷺ used to kiss her and suck her tongue when he was fasting.¹⁷¹

Aswad reported: "I and Masruq went to 'A'ishah and asked her if the Messenger of Allah ﷺ embraced (his wives) while fasting? She said: "Yes, but he had control over desire".¹⁷²

'Umar ibn Abu Salamah reported that he asked the Messenger of Allah ﷺ: "Can one observing the fast kiss his wife?" the Messenger of Allah ﷺ said to him: "Ask her (Umm Salamah)". She informed him that the Messenger of Allah ﷺ did that, whereupon he said: "Messenger of Allah, Allah pardoned you all your sins, the previous and the later ones". Upon this, the Messenger of Allah ﷺ said: "By Allah, I am the most Allah conscious among you and I fear Him most among you".¹⁷³

Abu Hurayrah narrated: "A man asked the Prophet ﷺ whether one who was fasting could embrace (his wife) and he gave him permission; but when another man came to him, and asked him, he forbade him. The one to whom he gave permission was an old man and the one whom he forbade was a youth".¹⁷⁴

WET DREAM

If one sleeps during the day and he had a wet dream or one looks at one's wife and thinks about sexual matters and has an emission, this does not affect one's fasting.¹⁷⁵ Abu Sa'id al-Khudri narrated that the

---

168 Al-Bukhari, *k. al-sawm, b. al-mubasharah li al-sa'im*; Muslim, *k. al-siyam, b. bayan anna al-qublah fi al-sawm laysat muharramah 'ala man lam tuharrik shahwatak*.
169 Muslim. *K. al-siyam, b. bayan anna al-qublah fi al-sawm laysat muharramah 'ala man lam tuharrik shahwatak*.
170 Abu Dawud, *k. al-siyam, b. al-qublah li al-sa'im*.
171 Abu Dawud, *k. al-sawm, b. al-sa'im yabla'u al-riq*.
172 Al-Bukhari, *k. al-sawm, b. al-mubasharah li al-sa'im*, Muslim, *k. al-siyam, b. bayan anna al-qublah fi al-sawm laysat muharramah 'ala man lam tuharrik shahwatak*.
173 Muslim, *k. al-siyam, b. bayan anna al-qublah fi al-sawm laysat muharramah 'ala man lam tuharrik shahwatah*.
174 Abu Dawud, *k. al-sawm, b. al-qublah li al-sa'im wa karahiyatihi li al-shabb*.
175 Al-Kasani, *Bada'i al-sana'i*, ii. 602.

Messenger of Allah ﷺ said: "Three things do not cause breaking of the fast: cupping, vomiting, and wet dreams".[176]

APPLYING OIL

It is allowed to apply oil, or drop oil or medicine in one's eyes.[177] However, if one drops medicine onto the nose or ear and it reaches the throat, this will break the fast.[178]

If drops are introduced into the penis this does not break the fast according to Abu Hanifah and Muhammad, while Abu Yusuf said that it does.[179]

COOLING WITH WATER

It is allowed for one to cool oneself in water or to put wet clothes on the body during fasting. Anas says: "I have a tub, in which I enter while I am fasting".[180] Abu Bakr ibn 'Abd al-Rahman, a Companion of the Prophet ﷺ, said: "I have seen the Apostle of Allah ﷺ in al-'Arj (name of a place between Madinah and Makkah) pouring water over hi head while he was fasting, either because of thirst or because of heat".[181] 'Abdullah ibn 'Umar moistened a cloth, then it was put on him while he was fasting.[182]

APPLYING KUHL

Kuhl is a black powder (antimony) applied to the eyes. It is allowed to apply *kuhl*. 'Aishah said that: "The Messenger of Allah ﷺ applied *kuhl* while he was fasting".[183] Anas reported that: "A man came to the Prophet ﷺ and said: 'My eye is hurting, can I apply *kuhl* while I am fasting?' He answered: 'Yes'."[184] A'mash says: "I did not see any of my teachers dislike *kuhl* for the fasting person".[185]

---

176 Al-Tirmidhi, *k. al-sawm, b. ma ja'a fi al-sa'im yadhra' uhu al-qay'*.
177 Al-Kasani, *Bada'i' al-sana'i'*, ii.606.
178 Ibid.
179 Al-Quduri, *al-Mukhtasar* 192.
180 Al-Bukhari, *k. al-sawm, b. ightisal al-sa'im*.
181 Abu Dawud, *k. al-siyam, b. al-sa'im yusabbu 'alayhi al-ma' min al-'atash...*
182 Al-Bukhari, *k. al-sawm, b. ightisal al-sa'im*.
183 Ibn Majah, *k. al-siyam, b. ma ja'a fi al-siwak wa al-kuhl li al-sa'im*.
184 Al-Tirmidhi, *k. al-sawm, b. ma ja'a fi al-kuhl li al-sa'im*.
185 Abu Dawud, *k. al-sawm, b. fi al-kuhl 'inda al-nawm li al-sa'im*.

INJECTION

Injections for medical reasons are allowed. Furthermore, it does not matter if what was injected reaches the stomach, as it does not reach the stomach through the customary manner (that food does).[186]

CUPPING

If one is subjected to cupping this does not break one's fast. 'Abdullah ibn 'Abbas narrated: "The Messenger of Allah ﷺ had himself cupped when he was fasting and wearing *ihram*".[187] Abu Sa'id al-Khudri narrated that the Messenger of Allah ﷺ said: "Three things do not cause the breaking of the fast: cupping, vomiting, and wet dreams".[188]

USING MISWAK OR TOOTHPASTE

Using miswak (a small twig for brushing teeth) is Sunnah during Ramadan throughout the day, as it is Sunnah during other days. 'Amir ibn Rabi'ah narrated: "I have seen the Apostle of Allah ﷺ more often than I could count, using a *miswak* while he was fasting".[189]

Similarly there is no harm in using toothpaste or tooth powder during fasting, as long as one makes sure they do not enter the throat.

---

186 See: *Fatawa Mustafa al-Zaraqa'* 173.
187 Al-Bukhari, *k. al-sawm, b. al-hijamah wa al-qay' li al-sa'im;* Muslim, *k. al-hajj, b. jawaz ul-hijamah li al—muhrim.*
188 Al-Tirmidhi, *k. al-sawm, b. ma ja'a fi al-sa'im yadhra'uhu al-qay'.*
189 Abu Dawud, *k. al-sawm, b. al-siwak li al-sa'im;* al-Tirmidhi, *k. al-sawm, b. ma ja'a fi al-siwak li al-sa'im.*

Chapter 7

WHAT BREAKS THE FAST

THOSE THINGS WHICH BREAK THE FAST
ARE OF TWO TYPES:
1. Those which break the fast and necessitate both *qada'* and *kaffarah*.
2. Those which break the fast and necessitate *qada'* only.

WHAT MAKES BOTH *QADA'* AND *KAFFARAH* COMPULSORY?

Qada' means to make up what has been missed. If what has been missed is the result of a wilful sin then, in addition, kaffarah (or expiation of the sin) is also required. For example, whoever deliberately has sexual intercourse or deliberately eats or drinks something – either to nourish himself or as a medicine – during the day in the fasting of Ramadan has committed a sin and nothing can compensate for it. Abu Hurayrah reported: "The Prophet ﷺ said: 'If anyone breaks his fast one day during Ramadan without a concession granted to him by Allah, a perpetual fast will not atone for it".[190]

Such a person must repent and must do both *qada'* and *kaffarah*.[191] *Qada'* is on account of the invalidation of his fast, and there is no difference of opinion in this. As for kaffarah, Abu Hurrayrah narrated: "While we were sitting with the Prophet ﷺ a man came and said: 'O Messenger of Allah! I have been ruined'. The Messenger of Allah ﷺ asked him what was the matter. He replied: 'I had sexual intercourse with my wife while I was fasting'. The Messenger of Allah ﷺ said to him: 'Can you afford to manumit a slave?' He replied in the negative. The Messenger of Allah ﷺ said to him: 'Can you fast for two successive

---

190 Abu Duwud, *k. al-sawm, b. al-taghliz fi man aftana 'amdan.*
191 Al-Samarqandi, *Tuhfat al-fuqaha'* 174.

months?' He replied in the negative. The Prophet ﷺ asked him: 'Can you afford to feed 60 poor people?' He replied in the negative. The Prophet ﷺ kept silent and while we were in that state, a big basket full of dates was brought to the Prophet ﷺ. He asked: 'Where is the questioner?' He replied: 'I (am here)'. The Prophet ﷺ said (to him): 'Take this (basket of dates) and give it in charity'. The man said: 'Should I give it to a person poorer than I?

By Allah; there is no family between its (i.e. Madinah's) two mountains who are poorer than I'. The Prophet ﷺ smiled until his premolar teeth became visible and then said: 'Feed your family with it'."[192]

Humayd ibn 'Abd al-Rahman reported that Abu Hurayrah had narrated to that the Messenger of Allah ﷺ commanded the person that broke the fast during Ramadan to free a slave or observe fasts for two (consecutive) months or feed 60 poor people. Imam Muhammad says after narrating this hadith: "We adhere to this, whoever breaks his fast deliberately during the month of Ramadan by eating or drinking or having sexual relations, has to do *qada'* of one day in its place and to do *kaffarah* of *zihar* (i.e. compensation as mentioned above in the hadith of Abu Hurayrah).[193] *Zihar* is the name of a particular oath common among the Arabs before the coming of Islam. This form of oath is strongly condemned in the Qur'an, especially when used as a form of divorce in the expression: "You are for me as the back of my mother".

Imam al-Zuhri says that anyone who eats deliberately during Ramadan is the same as one who has sexual relations with his wife, (i.e. he has to do *qada'* and *kaffarah* both).[194]

Smoking

Smoking tobacco (in whatever form) or chewing tobacco (in whatever form) are strongly disapproved at any time. However, if one deliberately consumes tobacco while fasting then it will break one's fast and one must offer both *qada'* and *kaffarah*.[195]

---

192 Al-Bukhari, *k. al-sawm, b.idha jama'a fi ramadan*; Muslim; *k. al-siyam, b. taghliz tahrim al-jima' fi nahar ramadan*.
193 Muhammad, *al-Mutwatta'*, 123.
194 'Abd al-Razzaq, *al-Musannaf*, iv.197.
195 *Hashiyat al-Tahtawi 'ala maraqi al-falah*, i. 364.

WHAT NECESSITATES QADA' ONLY?
The following necessitates *qada'*, but without any obligation to do *kaffarah*.

Breaking the fast by mistake
If one breaks one's fast by mistake one should continue the fast. There is no sin incurred but one has to do *qada'*.

If one gets up in the morning and believes that dawn has not broken and eats or breaks his fast considering that the sun has set, (and) then realises that dawn has broken or the sun has not set, one should continue fasting, and makes up that day, but does not have to do *kaffarah*.[196] Imam Muhammad narrates on the authority of Abu Hanifah from Ibrahim al-Nakha'i that: " 'Umar ibn al-Khattab and his companions broke the fast on a cloudy day thinking that the sun had set. Then the sun appeared. 'Umar said: 'We did not commit a sin, we will complete this day and will fast another in its place. Imam Muhammad says: "We adhere to this... and this is the opinion of Abu Hanifah".[197]

Breaking the fast for medical reasons
If one has begun a fast but then has an urgent need to take medication and taking that medication (this includes the use of inhalers). Breaks the fast, in such a case, one must do *qada'*, but not *kaffarah*.[198]

Restoring to medical treatment that does not entail anything that may be considered as taking food or drink will not break the fast: for example, if someone needs oxygen to assist their breathing.

Sexual contact that is less than jima'
Whoever has sexual contact but without *jima'* (penetration of the private parts) and ejaculates must make it up, but does not do *kaffarah*.[199]

If one has an emission as a result of kissing or touching, then he must make it up but he does not do *kaffarah*.[200]

---

196 Al-Quduri, *al-Mukhtasar* 196.
197 Abu-Hanifah, k. *al-athar* 71.
198 Al-Quduri, *al-Mukhtasar* 191.
199 Al-Samarqandi, *Tuhfat al-fuqaha'* 172.
200 Ibid.

Vomiting deliberately

If one is overcome by vomiting it does not break one's fast but if one induces vomiting and it fills one's mouth one must then make up the fast.[201] Abu Hurayrah narrated: "The Prophet ﷺ said: 'If one has a sudden attack of vomiting while one is fasting, no *qada'* is required of him, but if one vomits intentionally one must do *qada'*".[202] Imam Muhammad narrates on the authority of Abu Hanifah From Ibrahim al-Nakha'I about vomiting that there is no *qada'* on that person, except if one vomits deliberately, then in this case one has to complete the fasting and do the *qada'* later. Imam Muhammad says: "We adhere to this, and this is the opinion of Abu Hanifah".[203] 'Ali says: "If vomiting happens to someone, then there is no *qada'* on him, but if he vomits deliberately then there is *qada'* on him".[204] This is also the opinion of 'Abdullah ibn 'Umar, 'Alqamah, Hasan al-Basri, Muhammad ibn Sirin, 'Ata' ibn Abi Rabah, Qasim ibn Muhammad, 'Amir al-Sha'bi, Mujahid.[205]

Eating something which is not food

Whoever swallows a stone, or piece of iron or date stone breaks his fast and must make up the fast.[206]

Breaking a fast other than during the month of Ramadan

If one breaks his fast deliberately outside the month of Ramadan, whether it is obligatory fasting or voluntary then there is no *kaffarah* to pay, but one has to do *qada'*.[207] 'Aishah narrated: "Some food was presented to me and Hafsah. We were fasting, but broke our fast. Then the Apostle of Allah ﷺ entered upon us. We said to him: 'A gift was presented to us; we coveted it and we broke our fast'. The Apostle of Allah ﷺ said: 'There is no harm to you; keep a fast another day in lieu of it'."[208] Imam Muhammad says after narrating this hadith: "We adhere

---

201 Al-Quduri, *al-Mukhtasar* 190.
202 Abu Dawud, k. al-sawm, b. al-sa'im yastaqi'u 'amidan; al-Darimi, k. al-sawm, b. al-qay' li al-sa'im.
203 Abu Hanifah, k. *al-athar* 72.
204 Ibn Abi Shaybah, *al-Musannaf*, vi. 180.
205 Ibid, vi. 180-184.
206 Al-Samarqandi, *Tuhfat al-fuqaha'* 170.
207 Al-Kasani, *Bada'I al-sana'I*, ii. 625-6.
208 Abu Dawud, k. al-sawm, b. man ra'a 'alayh al-qada; al-Tirmidhi, k. al-sawm, b. ma ja'a fi ijab al-qada' 'alayh.

to this, whoever fasts voluntarily, and breaks it then he has to do *qada'*, and this is the opinion of Abu Hanifah".[209] 'Uthman al-Batti narrates that: "Anas ibn Sirin fasted on the day of 'Arafah, and became very thirsty, so he broke the fast. Then he asked a number of the Companions of the Prophet ﷺ. They commanded him to fast another day in its place".[210] 'Ata' ibn Abi Rabab narrates from Ibn 'Abbas that one has to fast another day in its place.[211]

DELAYING THE QADA'

One should do the *qada'* of fasting as soon as one is able to do so; but if one delays the *qada'* for a reason, then there is no sin for delaying. Abu Salamah reported: "I heard 'Aishah as saying: 'I had to complete some of the fasts of Ramadan, but I could not do it but during the month of Sha'ban due to my duties to the Messenger of Allah ﷺ or with the Messenger of Allah ﷺ".[212]

If one delays this until the next Ramadan begins, one fasts this second Ramadan and makes up the first afterwards and does not have to pay compensation. This is the opinion of Hasan al-Basri and Ibrahim al-Nakha'i.[213]

SEPARATION BETWEEN QADA' FASTS

In doing the *qada'* of Ramadan, a person may fast separate or consecutive days. Al-Hakam says: "Sa'id ibn Jubayr and Mujahid used to say: 'There is no harm in doing the *qada'* of Ramadan separately'."[214] Hasan al-Basri says: "There is no harm in doing the *qada'* of Ramadan separately as long as one counts the number of missed days".[215]

---

209 Muhammad, *al-Muwatta'* 127.
210 Ibn Abi Shaybah, *al-Musannaf*, vi. 161.
211 Ibid.
212 Al-Bukhari, k. al-sawm, b. mata yaqdi qada' ramadan; Muslim, k. al-siyam, b. qada' ramadan fi sha'ban.
213 Al-Baghawi, *Sharh al-sunnah*, iii. 507.
214 Ibid., iii. 508.
215 Ibid.

Chapter 8

THE NIGHT OF AL-QADR

THE NIGHT OF *aL-QADR* (Night of Decree) is the best and most auspicious night in the whole year. Allah, Exalted is He, says: "*Indeed, We sent the Qurʾan down during the Night of Decree. And what can make you know what the Night of Decree is? The Night of Decree is better than a thousand months. The angels and the Spirit descend therein by permission of their Lord for every matter. Peace it is until the emergence of dawn*".[216]

Imam Malik narrates: "The Messenger of Allah ﷺ was shown the lifespans of people who had gone before him. The Prophet looked at the shorter lifespan of his *ummah* and that they will not reach in deeds what others have reached due to the length of their lifespan. So Allah granted him the Night of *Qadr*, which is better than a thousand months".[217]

SEEKING THE NIGHT OF *AL-QADR*

It is recommended that one seeks for the Night of *Qadr*, especially during the month of Ramadan. ʿAishah has narrated that the Messenger of Allah ﷺ said: "Search for the Night of *Qadr* in the odd nights of the last ten days of Ramadan".[218] The Companions of the Prophet ﷺ the pious people of the later generations and Muslims all over the world have always made an effort to seek this night. The revelation of a whole surah (chapter) in the Qurʾan about this night and the concern of the Prophet ﷺ the Companions and people of the later generations leaves no doubt that this is the most important night of the whole year.

---

216 *Al-Qadr*.
217 Malik, al-Muwattaʾ, *k. al-Iʿtikaf, b. ma jaʾa fi laylat al-qadr*. Ibn ʿAbd al-Barr says: " I do not know of this been narrated anywhere other than *al-Muwattaʾ*, and this is one of those four *ahadith* which do not exist except in *al-Muwattaʾ*. (*al-Istidhkar*, x.342)
218 Al-Bukhari, *k. fadl laylat al-qadr, b. taharri laylat al-qadr fi al-witr min al-ʿashr al-awakhir*.

WHICH NIGHT IS IT?

There is a difference of the opinion among scholars as to which nights is the Night of *Qadr*. In what follows, I shall give the most important opinions in this regard:

1- Some people say that this night moves throughout the years; though mostly it is during Ramadan, nevertheless, it keeps changing every year. When the Qur'an was revealed, it was during Ramadan. That is the opinion of 'Abdullah ibn Mas'ud, Abu Hanifah, Abu Yusuf and Muhammad.[219]

2- Some say it is any night of the last ten nights of Ramadan. 'Aishah narrated: "The Messenger of Allah ﷺ used to do *i'tikaf* in the last ten nights of Ramadan and used to say: 'Look for the Night of *Qadr* in the last ten nights of the month of Ramadan'."[220] Abu Qilabah says: "The Night of *Qadr* moves across all ten nights".[221] That is the opinion of Malik, Sufyan al-Thawri, Shafi'I, Ahmad ibn Hanbal, Ishaq ibn Rahawayh and Abu Thawr.[222]

3- Some people say it is definitely the 27th night of Ramadan, Zirr ibn Hubaysh narrates: "I asked Ubayy ibn Ka'b: 'Your brother (in faith) Ibn Mas'ud says: 'He who stands for the night prayer throughout the year will find the Night of *Qadr*', whereupon, he said: 'May Allah have mercy upon him; he said these words with the intention that people might not rely only on one night, whereas he knew that it is during the month of Ramadan and it is the 27th night'. He then took an oath (without making any exception, i.e. without saying insha'Allah) that it was the 27th night. I said to him: 'Abu Mundhir, on what grounds do you say this?' Thereupon, he said: 'By the indication or by the sign which the Messenger of Allah ﷺ gave us, and that is that on that day (the sun) will rise without having any ray in it'."[223] Most people say it is any odd night during the last ten nights of Ramadan. 'Abdullah ibn 'Abbas narrates that the Prophet ﷺ said: "Look for the Night of *Qadr* during the last ten nights of Ramadan. 'Abdullah ibn 'Abbas narrates that the Prophet ﷺ said: "Look for the Night of *Qadr* during the last

---

219 Ibn 'Abd al-Barr, *al-Istidhkar*, x. 337.
220 Al-Bukhari, *k. fadl laylat al-qadr, b. taharri laylat al-qadr fi al-witr min al-'ashr al-awakhir*.
221 Ibn Abi Shaybah, *al-Musannaf*, vi .271.
222 Ibn 'Abd al-Barr, *al-Istidhkar*, x. 338.
223 Muslim, *k. al-siyam, b. fadl laylat al-qadr*.

ten days of Ramadan, on the night when nine or seven or five nights remain out of the last ten nights of Ramadan (i.e. 21, 23, and 25, respectively)".[224] 'Ubadah ibn al-Samit narrated: "The Prophet came out to inform us about the Night of *Qadr* but two Muslims were quarrelling with each other. So, the Prophet said: 'I came out to inform you about the Night of *Qadr* but so-and-so were quarrelling, so the news about it has been taken away; yet that might be for your own good, so search for it on the 29th, 27th and 25th (of Ramadan)".[225] Abu Sa'id al-Khadri narrated: "We did *i'tikaf* with the Messenger of Allah ﷺ in the middle ten days of Ramadan in the morning of the 20th he came out and (then) said: 'Whoever was in *i'tikaf* with me should remain in *i'tikaf* for the last ten days, for I was informed (of the date) of the Night *(of Qadr)* but I have been caused to forget it. (In the dream) I saw myself prostrating in mud and water in the morning of the night *(of Qadr)*. So, look for it in the last ten nights and in the odd ones of them'. It rained that night and the roof of the mosque dribbled as it was made from the leaf stalks of date-palms. I saw with my own eyes the mark of mud and water on the forehead of the Prophet (i.e. in the morning of the 21st)".[226] Abu Qibalah says: "The Night of *Qadr* moves in the odd nights of the last ten days of Ramadan".[227]

Shah Waliullah writes: "Know that the Night of *Qadr* is of two kinds: one is in which the Qur'an, the whole of it, was sent down to the firmament of the world, and, thereafter, was revealed little by little. This night comes only once in a year and it is also not necessary that it should be during the month of Ramadan. But, most probably, it is so. On the occasion of the revelation of the Qur'an, the night was during Ramadan. The other Night of *Qadr* is that in which a kind of spirituality is felt and the angels descend upon earth. The Muslims devote themselves to prayer during this night and they are benefited by each other's spiritual exaltation and blissfulness. The angels come close to them, the devils run away, and their devotions are accepted. The night occurs every year in the odd nights of the last ten days of Ramadan. It

---

224 Al-Bukhari, *k. fadl laylat al-qadr, b. taharri laylat al-qadr fi al-witr min al-'ashr al-awakhir.*
225 Al-Bukhari, *k. fadl laylat al-qadr, b. raj' ma'rifat laylat al-qadr...*
226 Al-Bukhari, *k. fadl laylat al-qadr, b. iltimas laylat al-qadr fi al-sab' alawakhir*; Muslim, *k. al-siyam, b. fadl laylat al-qadr.*
227 'Abd al-Razzaq, *al-Musannaf*, iv. 252.

can occur a little sooner or later, but it is always during the month of Ramadan. Thus, when a person speaks of the former Night of *Qadr* he says that it rotates in the year and when he speaks of the latter he says that it is found during the last ten days of Ramadan".[228]

WORSHIP DURING THIS NIGHT

'Aishah narrated that: "With the start of the last ten days of Ramadan, the Prophet ﷺ used to tighten his waist belt (i.e. work hard) and used to pray all the night, and used to keep his family awake for the prayers".[229]

'Aishah also said: "I asked the Messenger of Allah ﷺ if I know which night is the Night of *Qadr*, then what should I say in it? He answered: 'Say:

اللَّهُمَّ إِنَّكَ عَفُوٌّ تُحِبُّ الْعَفْوَ فَاعْفُ عَنِّى

'O Allah! Verily You are all-forgiving, You love forgiveness, so forgive me'."[230]

---

228 Al-Dihlawi, *Hujjatullah al-balighah*, ii. 85.
229 Al-Bukhari, *k. fadl laylat al-qadr, b. al-'amal fi al-awakhir min ramadan*; Muslim, *k. al-i'tikaf, b. al-ijtihad fi al-'ashr al-awakhir min ramadan*.
230 Al-Tirmidhi, *k. al-da'awat*; Ibn Majah, *k. al-du'a', b. al-du'a' bi al-'afw wa al-'afiyah*.

Chapter 9
I'TIKAF

I'TIKAF MEANS TO associate oneself with something, or to retire to devote oneself to it – be it good or bad. Allah, Exalted is He, says: "What are these statues to which you are devoted?"[231] – that which you are standing at and worshipping.

Here *I'tikaf* refers to staying in the mosque with the intention of attaining closeness to Allah, Exalted is He, while fasting.

I'tikaf is a completion of the benefits of the fasting. Ibn al-Qayyim writes: "The basic purpose of *i'tikaf* is that the heart gets attached to God, and with it, one attains inner composure and equanimity and preoccupation with the mundane things of life ceases and absorption in the Eternal Reality takes its place, and the state is reached in which all fears, hopes and apprehensions are superseded by the love and remembrance of God, every anxiety is transformed into anxiety for Him, and every thought and feeling is blended with the eagerness to gain His nearness and earn His good favour, and devotion to the Almighty is generated instead of devotion to the world and it becomes the provision for the grave where there will be neither a friend nor a helper. This is the high aim and purpose of *i'tikaf* which is the specialty of the most sublime part of Ramadan, i.e. the last ten days".[232]

Shah Waliullah remarks: "Since *i'tikaf* in the mosque is a means to the attainment of peace of the mind and purification of the heart, and it affords an excellent opportunity for forging an identity with the angels and having a share in the blissfulness of the Night of Power (Qadr) and for devoting oneself to prayer and meditation, Allah has set apart the last ten days of the month of Ramadan for it and made it a Sunnah

---

231 Al-Anbiya' 52.
232 Ibn al-Qayyim, *Zad al-ma'ad*, ii. 87.

for His pious and virtuous slaves".[233]

TYPES OF *I'TIKAF*
There are three types of *i'tikaf*:

1. Wajib *i'tikaf*
If one commits oneself to a certain number of days for *i'tikaf*, then it becomes *wajib (compulsory)* for one to make *i'tikaf* during the corresponding nights, while fasting. *Wajib i'tikaf* is not allowed without fasting.[234] 'Abdullah ibn 'Umar narrated: "Umar took a vow in the pre-Islamic days to spend a night or a day in devotion near the Ka'bah (in the sacred mosque). He asked the Prophet ﷺ about it. He said: "Observe *i'tikaf* (i.e. spend a night or a day near the Ka'bah) and fast'."[235]

Similarly if someone starts *i'tikaf* then it becomes *wajib* on him to complete it.[236]

2. Sunnah *i'tikaf*
I'tikaf in the last ten days and nights of Ramadan is Sunnah. Ubayy ibn Ka'b narrated: "The Prophet ﷺ used to observe *i'tikaf* during the last ten days of Ramadan. One year he did not observe *i'tikaf*. When the next year came, he observed *i'tikaf* for twenty nights (i.e. days)".[237] 'Abdullah ibn 'Umar reported that: "The Apostle of Allah ﷺ used to observe *i'tikaf* during the last ten days of Ramadan".[238] 'Aishah narrated: The Prophet ﷺ used to do *i'tikaf* during the last ten nights of Ramadan until he passed away. Then after him his wives did *i'tikaf*.[239]

---

233 Al-Dihlawi, *Hujjatullah al-balighah*, ii. 86.
234 Al-Kasani, *Bada'i al-sana'i*, iii 6-7.
235 Al-Bukhari, *k. al-i'tikaf, b. al-i'tikaf laylan*; Muslim, *k. al-ayman, b. nadhr al-kafir wa ma yaf alu fihi idha aslama*.
236 Al-Kasani, *Bada'i al-sana'i* , iii. 4.
237 Abu Dawud, *k. al-sawm, b. al-I'tikaf*; al-Tirmidhi, *k. al-sawm, b. ma ja'a fi al-I'tikaf idha kharaja minh*.
238 Al-Bukhari, *k. al-I'tikaf, b. al-b. al-I'tikaf fi al-'ashr al-awakhir*; Muslim, *k. al-I'tikaf, b. I'tikaf al-'ashr al-awakhir min ramadan*.
239 Al-Bukhari, k. al- *i'tikaf, b. al-I'tikaf fi al-'ashr al-awakhir*; Muslim, *k. al-I'tikaf, b. I'tikaf al-'ashr al-awakhir min ramadan*.

3. Mustahabb i'tikaf
Mustahabb i'tikaf can be done any time during the year.

CONDITIONS FOR THE VALIDITY OF *I'TIKAF*
Apart from the condition of Islam (i.e. being a Muslim) and sanity there are certain other conditions for I'tikaf to be valid. These are:

1. The person doing *i'tikaf* must be pure from *janabah*, *hayd* (menstruation) or *nifas* (postnatal bleeding) The reason that *i'tikaf* is not valid from an impure person is that *i'tikaf* is done on the mosque and an impure person is not allowed to enter into the mosque.[240] While being in *i'tikaf*, if one has a wet dream, then one must leave the mosque immediately, have a bath and return.

    If a women starts her period during *i'tikaf* she should cancel her *i'tikaf*, and do *qada'* later. Imam al-Zuhri says: "When a woman has her period during *i'tikaf*, then she should leave for her house, and when she becomes pure, she should do *qada'*".[241] The same has been narrated from Ibrahim al-Nakha'i, and 'Ata' ibn Abi Rabah.[242]

2. Intention is compulsory; because it is an act of worship, and an act of worship is not valid without the intention.[243]

3. Fasting. 'A'ishah has narrated the Prophet ﷺ said: "There is no *i'tikaf* without fasting".[244] 'Abdullah ibn 'Umar and 'Abdullah ibn 'Abbas said: "There is no *i'tikaf* without fasting".[245] 'A'ishah said: "Whoever does *i'tikaf*, he should fast".[246] This is the opinion of al-Zuhri and 'Urwah ibn al-Zubayr.[247]

In *nafl i'tikaf*, some people have allowed it to be for less than a day, in which case fasting will not be compulsory.[248]

---

240 Al-Kasani, *Bada'i al-sana'i*, iii. 5.
241 'Abd al-Razzaq, *al-Musannaf*, iv. 368.
242 Ibid., iv. 368-369.
243 Al-Kasani, *Bada'i al-sana'i*, iii. 6.
244 Al-Hakim, *al-Mustadrak*, k. al-sawm, b. al-I'tikaf; al-Daraqutni, *al-sunan*, k. al-siyam, b. al-I'tikaf; al-Bayhaqi, *al-sunan al-kubra*, k. al-siyam, b. al-mu'takif yasum.
245 'Abd al-Razzaq, al-Musannaf, iv. 353.
246 Ibid., iv. 354.
247 Ibid., iv. 354-355.
248 Al-Kasani, *Bada'I al-sana'I*, iii. 10.

It must be done in the *masjid* (mosque). Allah says: "But touch them not (that is, your wives) while you are in retreat (*i'tikaf*) in the mosques".[249]

4. According to Abu Hanifah, *i'tikaf* is not allowed except in a *masjid* in which the five daily prayers are performed.[250] Hudhayfah narrated that the Prophet ﷺ said: "Every mosque that has a caller to prayer and an imam is acceptable for *i'tikaf*".[251] Most people of knowledge, like Abu Hanifah, hold that *i'tikaf* is allowed in any (normally functioning) mosque. That is the opinion of 'A'ishah, Sa'id ibn Jubayr, Ibrahim al-Nakha'i, Abu Qilabah, al-Zuhri, al-Hakam, Hammad ibn Abi Sulayman, Malik and Shafi'i.[252] It is also the opinion of Abu Qilabah, Hammam ibn al-Harith, Abu Salamah ibn 'Abd al-Rahman, Abu al-Ahwas, al-Sha'bi, Sufyan al-Thawri, Ibn 'Ulayyah, Dawud al-Zahiri and Abu Ja'far al-Tabari.[253]

Women can do *i'tikaf* in the masjid of congregation if they want, or in the *masjids* of their house if they want.[254] Al-Athram says: "Ahmad ibn Hanbal was asked: 'Should women do *i'tikaf*? He said: 'Yes'."[255] The wives of the Prophet ﷺ did *i'tikaf* in the masjid, and they did not enter their homes except for human needs. 'A'ishah says: "I would enter into the house for human need, and if there was an ill person in the house, I would not ask about him except while I was passing".[256]

TIME
Wajib i'tikaf is for the days that one has committed oneself. It cannot be for less than a day.

Sunnah *i'tikaf* is for the last ten days of Ramadan. One will enter into the mosque before the sunset of 20th of Ramadan, and will stay

---

249 *Al-Baqarah* 187.
250 Ibid., iii. 18.
251 Al-Daraquini, *al-sunan, k. al-sawm, b. al-I'tikaf.*
252 Al-Baghawi, *Sharh al-sunnah*, iii. 551.
253 Ibn 'Abd al-Barr, *al-Istidhkar*, x. 274.
254 Al-Kasani, *Bada'I al-sana'I*, iii. 25.
255 Ibn 'Abd al- Barr, *al-Istidhkar*, x. 306.
256 Al-Bukhari, *k. al-I'tikaf, b. la yadkhulu al-bayta illa li hajah;* Muslim, *k. al-hayd, b. al-idtija' ma'a al-ha'id fi lihaf wahid.*

until the moon of *Shawwal* has been sighted.

Mustahabb i'tikaf can be undertaken at any time.

When one should go for the Sunnah i'tikaf
'A'ishah reported that when the Messenger of Allah ﷺ decided to observe *i'tikaf*, he prayed in the morning and then went to the place of his *i'tikaf*".²⁵⁷

SPECIFYING A PLACE THE MU'TAKIF
It is allowed for a *mu'takif* (one making *i'tikaf*) to make a specific place in the mosque for his *i'tikaf* as long as it does not harm or cause a major obstruction to the people coming for the congregational prayer. Abu Sa'id reported that the Prophet ﷺ performed *i'tikaf* under a Turkish tent which had something over its openings.²⁵⁸ 'Abdullah ibn 'Umar narrated that when the Prophet made *i'tikaf*, his bed would be placed behind the Pillar of Repentance (a pillar in the Prophet's mosque to which a Companion had tied himself until Allah accepted his repentance)".²⁵⁹

Nevertheless, if the imam fears that people specifying their places do not have good intention, or that it is going to harm the congregation, then he can stop people from doing so. 'A'ishah reported that when the Messenger of Allah ﷺ decided to observe *i'tikaf*, he prayed in the morning and then went to the place of his *i'tikaf*, and he commanded that a tent should be pitched for him, and it was pitched. He (once) decided to observe *i'tikaf* during the last ten days of Ramadan. Zaynab (the wife of the Prophet) commanded that a tent should be pitched for her. It was pitched accordingly. And some other wives of Allah's Apostle ﷺ commanded that tents should be pitched for them too. And they were pitched. When the Messenger of Allah ﷺ offered the morning prayer, he looked and found (so many) tents. Thereupon, he said: "What is this virtue that these (ladies) have decided to acquire?" He commanded his tent to be stuck and abandoned *i'tikaf* during the month of Ramadan and postponed it to the first ten days of *Shawwal*".²⁶⁰

---

257 Al-Bukhari, *k. al-I'tikaf, b. al-akhbiyah fi al-masjid*; Muslim, *k. al-I'tikaf, b. mata yadkhulu man arada al-I'tikaf fi mu'takafihi*.
258 Ibn Majah, *k. al-siyam, b. al-I'tikaf fi khaymat al-masjid*.
259 Ibn Majah, *k. al-siyam, b. fi- al-mu'takif yalzamu makanan fi al-masjid*.
260 Al-Bukhari, *k. al-I'tikaf, b. al-akhbiyah fi al-masjid*; Muslim, *k. al-I'tikaf, b. mata yadhkhulu man arada al-I'tikaf fi mu'takafihi*.

WHAT ONE SHOULD DO DURING I'TIKAF

The person doing *i'tikaf* should engage in acts of worship, like prayer, reading the Qur'an, remember of Allah, and reading useful books. One should only speak words of good and it is disliked for one to remain silent.[261]

'A'ishah reported that when the last ten nights began Allah's Messenger ﷺ kept awake at night (for prayer and devotion), awakened his family, and prepared himself to observe prayer (with more vigour).[262]

WHAT IS ALLOWED FOR THE MU'TAKIF

1. Leaving the mosque for human needs and Friday Prayer.[263] 'A'ishah reported: "When the Prophet ﷺ performed *i'tikaf*, he brought his head close to me so I could comb his hair, and he would nit enter the house except to fulfil the needs a person has".[264]
2. Eating and drinking in the mosque.[265]
3. Combing one's hair. As quoted above: 'A'ishah reported: "When the Prophet ﷺ performed *i'tikaf*, he brought his head close to me so I could comb his hair, and he would not enter the house except to fulfil the needs a person has".[266]
4. There is no harm in one selling or buying in the mosque but without bringing the goods with one.[267]

WHAT INVALIDATES THE I'TIKAF

1. It is forbidden for the one in the *i'tikaf* to have sexual intercourse, touch a woman, kiss and if one has an emission as a result of kissing or touching then one's *i'tikaf* is invalidated and must be made up.[268] Allah, Exalted is He, says: "*But touch them not [that is, your wives] while you are in retreat (i'tikaf) in the mosques*".[269]

---

261 Al-Quduri, *al-Mukhtasar* 198.
262 Muslim, *k. al-I'tikaf, b. al-ijtihad fi al-'ashr al-awakhir min shahr ramadan*.
263 Al-Samarqandi, *Tuhfat al-fuqaha'* 181.
264 Al-Bukhari, *k. al-I'tikaf, b. la yadkhulu al-bayta illa li hajah*; Muslim, *k. al-hayd, b. jawaz ghasl al-ha'id ra'sa zawjiha wa tarjilih*..
265 Al-Samarqandi, *Tuhfat al-fuqaha'* 181.
266 Al-Bukhari, *k. al-I'tikaf, b. la yadkhulu al-bayta illa li hajah*; Muslim, *k. al-hayd, b. jawaz ghasl al-ha'id ra'sa zawjiha wa tarjilih* ...
267 Al-Quduri, *al-Mukhtasar* 198.
268 Al-Kasani, *Bada'i al-sana'i*, iii. 31.
269 *Al-Baqarah* 187.

Touching one's wife without there being any desire is allowed. For example, the statement of 'A'ishah cited earlier whereby she would comb the Prophet's hair while he was performing *i'tikaf*.

2. Loss of reason from intoxicants or becoming insane.
3. The start of menstruation or post-childbirth bleeding.[270]
4. If one goes out of the mosque for a while without an excuse, then one's *i'tikaf* is invalidated, according to Abu Hanifah, while Abu Yusuf and Muhammad both said that it is not invalidated unless he is away for more than half a day.[271]

'A'ishah says: "It is Sunnah on the *mu'takif* that he does not visit an ill person, does not attend funeral prayers, does not touch a woman, does not embrace her, and does not embrace her, and does not go out except for absolute necessity. There is no *i'tikaf* without fasting, and there is no *i'tikaf* but in a congregational mosque".[272] The same has been narrated from al-Zuhri, 'Ata' ibn Abi Rabah, and 'Urwah ibn al-Zubayr.[273] It is reported by 'Amrah that 'A'ishah, while in *i'tikaf* would go to her house for human need and she would pass by an ill person, and would ask about him while passing but without stopping.[274] Abu Salamah ibn 'Abd al-Rahman says: "The *mu'takif* when entering into the house (for human need) would say *salam*, and can visit the ill without sitting".[275]

QADA' OF I'TIKAF

It is obligatory for a person to do the *qada'* of a Sunnah or *mustahab i'tikaf* if they do not complete it after having made the intention.[276]

As stated in 'A'ishah's earlier hadith that the Messenger of Allah ﷺ once abandoned his *i'tikaf* during the month of Ramadan and postponed it to the first ten days of *Shawwal*".[277]

Imam al-Tirmidhi says: "There is a difference of opinion about a

---

270 Ibid., iii. 5.
271 Al-Quduri, *al-Mukhtasar* 199.
272 Abu-Dawud, *k. al-sawm, b. al-mu'takif ya'ud al-marid*.
273 'Abd al-Razzaq, *al-Musannaf*, iv. 357-360.
274 Ibid., iv. 358.
275 Ibid.
276 Al-Kasani, *Bada'i al-sana'i*. iii. 4-5.
277 Al-Bukhari, *k. al-I'tikaf, b. al-akbiyah fi al-masjid*; Muslim, *k. al-I'tikaf, b. mata yadkhulu man arada al-I'tikaf fi mu'takafihi*.

person who ends his *i'tikaf* before his intended time has expired. Some people of knowledge say: 'If he ends his *i'tikaf* [early], it is obligatory upon him to make it up'. They use as proof the hadith which states that when the Prophet abandoned his *i'tikaf*, he made it up during the following month of *Shawwal*. This is the opinion of Malik".[278]

---

278 Al-Tirmidhi, k. al-sawm, b. ma ja'a fi al-I'tikaf idha kharaja minhu.

ALSO AVAILABLE BY LIGHT PUBLISHING

ALSO AVAILABLE BY LIGHT PUBLISHING

www.ingramcontent.com/pod-product-compliance
Lightning Source LLC
Chambersburg PA
CBHW011127070526
44584CB00028B/3815